Posttraumatic Nightmares

POSTTRAUMATIC NIGHTMARES
Psychodynamic Explorations

Melvin R. Lansky
with Carol R. Bley

THE ANALYTIC PRESS

1995   Hillsdale, NJ   London

Published by
The Analytic Press, Inc.
365 Broadway
Hillsdale, New Jersey 07642

The following chapters were published previously and appear here, in revised
form, by permission of their copyright owners: ch. 2—British Journal of Psychotherapy (1990, 6:384-400); ch. 3—Hillside Journal of Clinical Psychiatry (1989,
11:169-183); ch. 4—Bulletin of the Menninger Clinic (1991, 55:104-110); ch. 5—
Bulletin of the Menninger Clinic (1991: 55:470-490); ch. 6—Dreaming (1992,
2:99-109); ch. 7—Dreaming (1992, 3:21-31); ch. 8—Bulletin of the Menninger
Clinic (1995, 59:1-11); ch. 10—Bulletin of the Menninger Clinic (1990, 54:466-
477).

Typeset in Garamond by TechType, Upper Saddle River, NJ

Library of Congress Cataloging-in-Publication Data

Lansky, Melvin R.
   Posttraumatic nightmares : psychodynamic explorations / Melvin R.
   Lansky, with Carol R. Bley.
         p.   cm.
   Includes bibliographical references and index.
   ISBN 0-88163-193-0
   1. Post-traumatic stress disorder.   2. Nightmares.   3. Psychic
   trauma.   I. Bley, Carol R. II. Title.
RC552.P67L36 1994
616.85'21—dc20   94-43415
                                                            CIP

Printed in the United States of America
10 9 8 7 6 5 4 3 2 1

For Karen, Madeleine, and Joshua

"Oh God, I could be bounded in a nutshell and
count myself a king of infinite space,
were it not that I have bad dreams."
[*Hamlet* II, ii 251–252]

Acknowledgments

Integrative work draws from many sources. I owe many debts of thanks to those who have expanded my knowledge of dream dynamics, of family systems, and of shame. The investigations from which this study arose were made possible by the confluence of what, for several decades, had been my deep immersion in two very different worlds of clinical practice and two very different academic affiliations.

The first world is that of the private practice of psychoanalysis and psychoanalytic psychotherapy, a practice that informs my scholarly activities at the Los Angeles Psychoanalytic Institute. This world of minute attention to the intrapsychic experiences and defensive operations of patients seen individually and intensively over a lengthy period is the setting in which the study of dreams and of dream analysis comes naturally to the fore. I benefited greatly from Leo Rangell's insightful discussion of my presentation of what is now chapter 2 of this book. I have for many years, in the course of teaching seminars on dreams, discussing clinical material and participating in study groups both formal and informal, learned much about dreams from my psychoanalytic colleagues, Drs. Richard Baker, Allan Compton, Richard Fox, Malcolm Hoffs, Benjamin Kilborne, and Jeffrey Levine.

The second world was that of my experience as founder and director of a UCLA teaching service, the Family Treatment Program, a 20-bed psychiatric ward at the West Los Angeles VA Medical Center. This academic post gave me the opportunity to study closely a wide variety of very seriously disturbed persons evaluated both in terms of underlying dynamics and in the context of their families. It is this setting that provided the unique opportunities for the in-depth study of almost 200 nightmare sufferers over a period of seven years. I am grateful to enlightened superiors both at the hospital and in the UCLA Department of Psychiatry who, in the face of complex academic priorities and fiscal limitations, gave the program the support and encouragement that allowed clinical, educational, and investigative efforts to continue for more than two decades. I am indebted more than I can say to colleagues in the Family Treatment Program— comrades-in-arms too numerous to list separately here. They made the day-to-day work vibrant and meaningful. Judith Karger was my talented and valued collaborator for the first year of the study, the work that comprises chapters 2 and 3. Howard Fishbein added much to chapter 10 on nightmares and substance abuse. I especially thank two sustaining, nurturant, and clinically gifted presences of the Family Treatment Program: Geneva McVey, head nurse of the program throughout its entire existence, and Carol Bley, Program Coordinator, collaborator, and friend, who contributed her dedication, insightfulness, and great clinical skills to the interviewing, follow up, and discussion of each patient and each written publication for six of the seven years that the study was in progress.

A central vision that permeates the whole of the study concerns the role of shame in predisposing vulnerabilities, instigation of the nightmares, and coexisting trauma contemporaneous with the scene of the posttraumatic nightmare scenario. Drs. Jack Katz, Benjamin Kilborne, Andrew Morrison, Suzanne Retzinger, Thomas Scheff, and Léon Wurmser have deepened my appreciation of shame dynamics and shame conflicts in countless conversations over many years.

I would like to offer special thanks to the staff at The Analytic Press—Joan Riegel, Eleanor Starke Kobrin, and especially Dr. Paul Stepansky, who, once again with this book, encouraged and assisted me in every way in its conception, evolution, and writing.

Lastly, and most emphatically, I wish to express my gratitude to the nightmare sufferers who shared with me the agony and heartbreak that I have tried to capture in the pages that follow. They hope, as do I, that exploration and greater understanding of their nightmares will pave the way to more effective treatment.

Los Angeles, California
October 1994

Contents

Foreword

Bennett Simon

"The making of many books is a weariness of the flesh, my son," admonishes the author of Ecclesiastes, undoubtedly himself discouraged by the relatively indifferent reception to his own writings sometime and somewhere in ancient Israel. But this book by Melvin Lansky is definitely not among the "weariness" works: it is a book that takes *risks*. Let me cite some of the risks it takes.

First of all, it is a book filled with the most awful traumatic material—the nightmares vie with the recollections of actual trauma, combat and intrafamilial, over which is more "nightmarish." Consider the nightmare reported in chapter 5, which includes a narrative about the dreamer, an 18-year-old medic, helping debride a horribly burned Vietnamese child. "The smell and stink—it was horrible. The doctor came in to check the child's ears and eyes. I said, 'No.' I lifted up the eyelids. The eyes were like white jelly. They were burned out. The smell. I went outside and puked, then came back in and debrided." A few lines later the author inserts the terse notice that "this scene had actually occurred." The patient's nightmares also incorporate elements of his witnessing a group of American soldiers brutally

Bennett Simon, M.D. is Clinical Professor of Psychiatry, Harvard Medical School (at the Cambridge Hospital); Training and Supervising Analyst, Boston Psychoanalytic Society and Institute; and Co-Director, "Children-in-War" project, Cambridge Hospital.

humiliating, beating, and killing an elderly Vietnamese man who had offered them a basket of fruit. The risk here is that the reader can easily turn off or turn away from such material. No one should have to live through such horrors, either as a victim, as a perpetrator, or as a witness. No one should have to hear such stories. It is not right, not fair, and not what most of us were brought up to expect, either in our childhood experiences or in much of our mental health training— except that our reading of the daily newspapers tells us that the nightmares are all too real. But the book succeeds in allowing us to continue reading, to resume the work of debriding, as it were, even though we may have to vomit.

The second risk in this book is that the author has relied heavily on facts, however shaky and slippery, of clinical interviews and clinical assessments. Linus Pauling was quoted as having said something like, "If I have to choose between a fact and a theory, I'll choose the theory, because facts can be proven wrong." Lansky and his co-workers interviewed Vietnam veterans in the VA hospital, used questionnaires, interviewed and worked with the families of many of the veterans, followed the course of the treatment of these men, and thereby collected a great deal of data. Now the risk is, as they are aware, that "facts can be disproven." They have a highly selected group of patients, not at all representative of other trauma victims and of other types of trauma, not representative of the different person-ality styles and different diagnoses that characterize "trauma vic-tims." The investigators' inquiries might have been hopelessly biased and contaminated by their hypotheses; their patients highly suggest-ible, compliant, or skilled at sustaining the interest of investigators and therapists. These are the risks you take if you rely on actually talking to a significant number of people and not writing a single case report, however loosely detailed, and however subtle, but only speculating. Lansky, citing his progenitors and colleagues in this work, carefully attempts to distill out what is essential and what is durable in the work of others and yet clearly and forthrightly states his differences from them.

The third risk in this work is that Lansky attempts to examine theories about traumatic nightmares, including psychoanalytic theo-ries, and thereby wrestles with the proverbial 800-pound marshmal-low. In an age when simple formulations and simple treatments are in high demand, he offers complex, but not dense and impenetrable, theoretical formulations and reformulations. His emphasis on the role of shame and humiliation in the genesis and perpetuation of traumatic nightmares is an example of a convincing and innovative formulation, leading to greater conceptual clarity and, more important, to greater therapeutic success.

Overall, he treads an area—traumatic stress studies—that is highly contested territory, where psychoanalysis in particular is on the defensive, where there are literal and metaphorical lobbies of different treatment approaches and of different groups of victims. This is an area where to claim, as Lansky does, that the nightmares and flashbacks of his patients are not only and not always veridical representations of actual combat trauma, but condensations with prewar and with postwar traumas and humiliations, is not entirely neutral. Those who worked in the task of interviewing Holocaust survivors for purposes of substantiating their claims for reparations from the German government remember that for a period of time some German psychiatrists and courts were arguing (and, to her horror, citing the writings of Anna Freud!) that the personality is formed by age six or that many who suffered in the camps were already damaged personalities before their concentration-camp experience. Any work that points to earlier life traumatic experiences runs the risk of being denounced as "blaming the victim" or as actually or potentially supporting governmental refusal to pay compensation.

One more risk: Lansky states that he may not know it all, that what he has discovered and formulated may be only part of the truth, and he put his work in a form that is accessible and ultimately in significant measure testable. He is clear about what the contributions of himself and his colleagues are, but modest and judicious in claims they make vis-à-vis other modes of understanding and of treatment.

Let me highlight some ramifications of the work reported herein. A younger colleague, treating a young woman about whom there is a question as to whether or not she was sexually abused during her preadolescent years, reports some of her dreams, leading us to a discussion of the relationships among memory, dreaming, and trauma. He stops as he recollects that his father, who had been a prisoner of war in World War II, spoke little of his wartime experiences but had recurrent nightmares, with loud vocalizations. For the young child, born after the war, these nightly recurrences were for a period of years a permanent and expectable feature of family life. Clearly, a major means of the father's communicating the depth and terror of his experiences was the nightmare. Or, consider Shakespeare's account of the nightmares of Harry Percy in Henry IV, Part I, and their impact on Percy's wife. She complains to him that he has been withdrawn and melancholic. She beseeches, "For what offence

have I this fortnight been / A banish'd woman from my Harry's bed?''
She describes how,

> In thy faint slumbers I by thee have watch'd,
> And heard thee murmur tales of iron wars;
> Speak terms of manage to thy bounding steed;
> Cry "Courage! to the field!" And thou hast talk'd
> Of sallies and retires, of trenches, tents, . . .
> Of prisoners' ransomes and of soldiers slain.
> And all the currents of a heady fight.
> Thy spirit within thee hath been so at war
> And thus hath so bestirr'd thee in thy sleep,
> That beads of sweat have stood upon thy brow,
> Like bubbles in a late-disturbed stream;
> And in thy face strange motions have appear'd
> Such as we see when men restrain breath
> On some great sudden hest. O, what portents are these?
> Some heavy business hath my lord in hand,
> And I must know it, else he loves me not [2.3.36–64].

She simultaneously fears for his life, is distressed at his distress, fears the loss of his love, and knows and yet does not know what is at hand in terms of the next battle.

Finally, recall that the perpetrator can also experience the nightmarish and hallucinatory disturbances of sleep that are encapsulated in Macbeth's famous lines after he has slain the sleeping king, Duncan, "Methought I heard a voice cry, 'Sleep no more! Macbeth does murder sleep' "(2.2.49–50).

What all these instances convey is that the disturbances of sleep associated with traumatic intrusions have a major communicative and affective impact on those around the dreamer. Indeed, one colleague, Gilbert Kliman (personal communication), has speculated that there is an evolutionary group-survival value in traumatic nightmares—they communicate the fact of terrible danger to those in the group around the traumatized dreamer. But what is clear to all is that these nightmares, however engendered, are part of the interpersonal and affective world of the one who suffers the nightmares—no one dreams alone. They also become major communications from patient to therapist, especially if we take seriously Ferenczi's (1912) brief paper "To Whom Does One Relate One's Dreams?"—the person to whom you tell the dream is an association to the dream. Lansky elaborates how multiple traumatic life experiences, complex wishes, fears, defenses, and compromises are condensed and conveyed to the dreamer and to the audience, who may hear middle-of-the-night shrieks or be told the narrated dream in an office in the daylight.

My own interests in the long-term impact of war and violence on young children lead me also to paraphrase Lansky's formulations to emphasize the proposition that the nightmare represents an *intergenerational phenomenon*. Containing the history of the dreamer's traumatic experiences with his parents, dreams often reflect the parents' experience with their own parents and at the same time communicate the terrible stories and experiences to the next generation. The nightmare is thus a condensation of what has happened, what is happening, and what can happen, internally and externally, over several generations. This perspective is implicit in the *modus operandi* of Lansky and his colleagues in their emphasis on family interviewing and working with families as well as with the patients. Terrible things that people do to one another, especially to children and other highly vulnerable groups, are indelibly recorded in these nightly annals, and carry a heading, "Lest we forget, however hard we are also trying to forget!"

In this sense, I would locate Lansky's work on nightmares not only alongside his own previous work on *Fathers Who Fail* (Lansky, 1992) but also with other studies of the intergenerational transmission of trauma. I have in mind, as an exemplary exploratory work, the forthcoming book by Israeli psychologist Dan Bar-On (in press), *Between Fear and Hope: Three Generations of the Holocaust*. Another way to phrase Lansky's psychodynamic accounts of how the nightmares are formed and experienced is that we have an opportunity to study not only the harmful effects of transmitted trauma, but the variety of ways in which individuals try to master and even transmute the trauma. We may then, have another window into the mysteries of the resilience of so many trauma victims and their children.

The results of the study reported in this book also have important implications for treatment of patients who are suffering from recurrent nightmares or recurrent or chronic posttraumatic states. First of all, the book makes an important contribution to differentiating patient groups and to our thinking about how the nightmare experience might be utilized by different diagnostic groups. The finding that borderline patients were eager and able to use their narrations and discussions of their nightmares in the service of recovery is striking and important. It is an extension of a principle that needs continually to be rediscovered and reaffirmed—good clinical investigation and research can also be enormously therapeutic! The emphasis on the role of shame and humiliation in the dynamics of nightmare formation also appears to me to open wider possibilities in the treatment of "stuck" patients. Augmenting what others have found in terms of helplessness, aggression, and highly eroticized sadomasochistic themes, it adds to our catalogue of what may be entailed in persistent posttraumatic states.

Second, I believe that by calling attention to the detailed study of patients with these nightmares, the book constitutes a call to other therapists and clinical investigators to review and rethink their own work and also sets up a model for others to collect data that may confirm, supplement, or disconfirm Lansky's findings. The data on the complex relationship between the "manifest" and "latent" content of the nightmare are most impressive, and they keep open important debates on the nature of posttraumatic states. The investigation of flashbacks, slip dreams, and sleep phobias opens up fresh channels of investigation. The book thus is an appeal for an open mind, to avoid a race toward premature closure on theoretical and therapeutic issues.

Finally, the book is one of the more creative efforts to come to terms with the terrible deeds and consequences of the Vietnam War. The investigations and therapies reported in this book represent a mixture of clear-eyed intelligence, great diligence, and great compassion in attempting to face and heal the wounds of the war. It demonstrates the courage of those who are willing, as it were, to put themselves in the line of fire in working with the tortured minds and bodies of victims and victimizers. It is a testimony also to the kind of commitment both by mental health professionals and by the institutions within which they work that is needed to work long-term with the consequences of massive trauma caused by war and persecution. It must be read by those who work extensively and intensively with trauma victims and by those (including many psychoanalysts) who have not had or have eschewed the opportunities to work with trauma victims. It shows to all who are willing to see how war adds to the burdens of those already traumatized, that putting the "already traumatized" in war may pave the way for some of them to commit atrocities (thus creating whole new waves of traumatized people), and for exacerbating the traumatic wounds of many others. Therefore, the contents of this book must be noted by those in our professional societies and in our government empowered to determine the policies and allocate finances in deciding how we attempt to hurt and how we attempt to heal.

REFERENCES

Bar-On, D. (in press), *Between Fear and Hope: Three Generations of the Holocaust*. Cambridge, MA: Harvard University Press.

Ferenczi, S. (1912), To whom does one relate one's dreams? In: *Further Contributions to the Theory and Technique of Psycho-analysis*, ed. J. Rickman (trans. J. Suttie). London: Karnac Books, 1980.

Lansky, M. (1992), *Fathers Who Fail: Shame and Psychopathology in the Family System*. Hillsdale, NJ: The Analytic Press.

PART I

INTRODUCTION

CHAPTER 1

Trauma and Nightmare

I

Trauma sufferers have nightmares. Trauma, whether it be from a natural disaster, such as a hurricane or an earthquake; from a car or train accident; or from an attack by abusive parents, a rapist, a mugger, enemy soldiers, or concentration camp guards, is very commonly followed by terrifying anxiety dreams. These dreams seem, in the dreamer's experience and when told to others, to be so intimately related to the traumatic event that questions about the relation of trauma to dream are often not asked, much less answered. Dreams of this sort are often thought of as more or less like an inflammatory response that follows an injury, that is, simply and unquestionably part of the entire picture of injury and response to it. In fact, in most of the literature on trauma— even in the psychoanalytic literature—traumatic nightmares are not conceptualized as true dreams with latent content that differs from the manifest content, often significantly, resulting from the operations of dream work, with condensation, displacement, and symbol formation and from secondary revision; serving a defense function; and under the influence, however subtle, of wish fulfillment. Applied to the problem of posttraumatic nightmares, the wish fulfillment hypothesis is particularly counterintuitive: how can one imagine the return to a scene that is, by definition, traumatic to the point of generating overwhelming and unmanageable terror? Small wonder, then, that dream dynamics

3

specific to posttraumatic nightmares are seldom studied as true dreams by trauma researchers. Nightmares rarely occur in sleep laboratories (Fisher et al., 1970) and so are seldom directly studied by sleep researchers.

In the analytic or psychotherapeutic situation, the circumstance in which dreams are presumably best and most rigorously studied, the prevalence of actual posttraumatic nightmares in the practice of any given analyst is likely to be small. Furthermore, the analyst or therapist is not likely to respond to a recently traumatized person's report of an anxiety dream with systematic dream analysis, especially if that patient says, as trauma victims so commonly do, that the dreams are "just about what happened." Even in the analytic situation, then, there is some likelihood either that posttraumatic nightmares will not be treated as true dreams or that the experience of any one analyst with posttraumatic nightmares per se is likely to be minimal.

Whatever the combination and despite the fact that the association of trauma with nightmares has become, in the common consciousness, a truism, the study of posttraumatic nightmares as true dreams is (with a few notable exceptions) strikingly sparse. In the common view, the posttraumatic nightmare takes place soon after the trauma, repeats the traumatic situation virtually exactly, and disappears or blends in with normal dream elements in a matter of weeks or months (Hartmann, 1984). The posttraumatic nightmare is viewed, more like an affectively laden memory—more like a nighttime flashback than like a true dream. Such a view of the posttraumatic nightmare, explicit or implicit, is the prevailing one.

But a closer look suggests that things are more complex than the state of affairs implied by the prevailing view of posttraumatic nightmares. Weiss and Sampson (1986) report a study in which released prisoners of war reported three types of traumatic dreams. Prior to capture they dreamed of being invaded and overrun by enemy troops. These dreams could be seen as preparatory to battlefield danger. They were, in effect, compromise formations actualizing the need for the dreamer both to sleep and to be vigilant in the face of likely attack. During confinement, these prisoners often dreamed of comfortable living situations and pleasant meals. Only after their return to the United States did they dream about combat, the death of comrades, and capture.

Writing of his World War II clinical experiences in Guadalcanal, Lidz (1946) noted a strikingly high prevalence of early familial trauma in those soldiers who had the most severe combat nightmares. He pointed to their conscious hatred of their fathers, perhaps related to the unconscious suicidal wishes so evident in their posttraumatic nightmares. Another striking finding in Lidz's study was the high prevalence of coexisting trauma—buddies dying, "Dear John" letters received—reported by the soldiers with the most severe posttraumatic reactions. Moses (1978) also, writing of posttraumatic reactions among Israeli soldiers, has noted that the most severely affected soldiers had a striking prevalence of early familial trauma.

The nine chapters that form the clinical heart of this book grew out of a seven-year study (1987-1993) of patients admitted to an inpatient psychiatric unit at the West Los Angeles VA Medical Center. The study, limited to psychiatric inpatients, draws from a confluence of interests that include the psychoanalytic study of dreams, an intergenerational focus on family systems, and a general psychiatric symptomatology understood from the point of view of narcissistic equilibrium in family systems, with special emphasis on the role of shame in symptom formation (Lansky, 1977, 1984).

Clinical work in our study gave our research group the opportunity to appreciate the complexity of the posttraumatic nightmare. Consider the following clinical situations.

> A Vietnam combat veteran who says that his dreams are simply about the war reports a dream in which he shoots an attacking Viet Cong soldier on a roof. The soldier falls dead and the patient recognizes him as his own brother (chapter 3).

> A man admitted a few days after a surprise shooting in which his friend, probably a drug dealer, is shot to death by two men reports a dream in which a woman, rather than the two assailants, approaches his car and calls him by his (unusual) first name (chapter 2).

> A man homosexually raped in prison has his first posttraumatic nightmare 12 years later at a time when his wife threatens to leave him (chapter 6).

> A rape victim hospitalized shortly after the rape dreams that the rapist himself has been admitted to the same (mostly male) hospital (chapter 8).

These and many other clinical situations cry out for a better understanding of posttraumatic nightmares than we now have.

This book attempts a clinically useful, psychoanalytically informed conceptualization of posttraumatic nightmares that emphasizes the function of those nightmares. It derives from a detailed, clinical understanding of nightmare sufferers at a veterans hospital in

Southern California. They arise not only from research, interviews, and psychotherapy sessions alone, but also from detailed observations of nightmare sufferers in the context of close ward observation and almost always in the context of an intergenerational family workup that is a part of the evaluation and treatment of every patient admitted to the ward on which these studies were made.

These reports are presented here in an order that emphasizes features related to the *function* of posttraumatic nightmares. The emphasis on function should not be taken lightly since it is far from clear, given the existing literature on the subject, and perhaps begs the question to assume that posttraumatic nightmares have any function at all. Psychoanalytically, of course, the issue of function of dreams is often felt to center on the wish-fulfillment hypothesis—a hypothesis that underwent its most serious scrutiny and continued controversy over the very topic of posttraumatic nightmares.

The central line of thinking that unites the clinical chapters of the book does indeed support a revised concept of wish fulfillment, one that draws heavily on an understanding of shame, narcissistic injury, and narcissistic rage and their relation to disruptive mental states in the light of which even the possession of an intact sense of self within the scenario of a terrifying anxiety dream can be seen as a wish.

The reports are grouped in such a way as to highlight three features of posttraumatic nightmares usually ignored or underemphasized, even in psychoanalytic studies: *latent content* (or the screening function) of the dreams, so commonly and erroneously thought to be simple replays of a traumatic scene; *instigation* of the dream, commonly ignored or assumed to be a reaction either to the trauma itself or to nonspecific stress; and the *relation of the nightmare to the impaired or traumatized psyche*.

The immediate clinical context of this study, embedded as it was in the treatment situation in an inpatient psychiatric unit, offers, in addition to the obvious sample bias toward seriously disturbed nightmare sufferers, the advantage of an unusually perspicuous focus on the counterpoint between the dreamer's manifest nightmare and the interpersonal and interfamilial matrix with which that dreamer has struggled, often lifelong. We found (chapter 3), in addition to the trauma in the nightmare scenario, a consistent series of lifelong traumata in the lives of our posttraumatic nightmare sufferers. These traumata include predisposing childhood trauma, trauma contemporaneous with the trauma in the dream—usually some sort of narcissistic wounding—and trauma resulting from current familial or interpersonal dysfunction. Although it may be argued that our sample is highly biased in favor of unusually traumatized and dysfunctional persons, observations drawn from other settings confirm our emphasis on factors that predispose toward severe posttraumatic states and posttraumatic nightmares (Lidz, 1946; Moses, 1978).

The confluence of intensive clinical embeddedness with a clinical and theoretical interest in dreams and nightmares, the role of shame in symptom formation, and the intergenerational study of the regulation of familial narcissistic equilibrium combine in the pages that follow to give a view of posttraumatic nightmares that is more clinically comprehensive than are those drawn from theory alone, those drawn from trauma research outside the context of treatment, or those drawn or extrapolated from the methods of sleep research outside of the clinical purview entirely.

II

Posttraumatic nightmares can be considered from psychodynamic viewpoints, from cognitive-behavioral viewpoints, from the point of view of laboratory investigations of sleep and dreams, and from the point of view of the investigation of trauma.

Psychodynamic considerations of posttraumatic nightmares begin, of course, with Freud. Freud (1900) emphasized that the problem with nightmares or anxiety dreams generally was not so much one for the theory of dreams as it was for the theory of anxiety. The anxiety dream, seen as a reflection both of an unconscious wish and of the reaction to that wish, reflected a conflictual situation that, purely and simply, gave rise to too much anxiety for the dream to handle, and, for this reason, the nightmare evidenced a failure of the sleep-protecting function of dreams. The principle of wish fulfillment, the basic function of the dream, that is, as an attempt to modulate affect and tension by representing a wish as fulfilled, is not necessarily contradicted by the existence of anxiety dreams.

Matters became more complicated, of course, when Freud's younger colleagues, serving in World War I, pointed to problems for the theory of dreams posed by specifically posttraumatic anxiety dreams related to combat experiences. These colleagues, like Freud himself, presumed somewhat offhandedly that such posttraumatic nightmares were in fact simple replays of the traumatic event, more like memories than true dreams.

Since the dream was presumably about the trauma, there seemed to be almost by definition, no latent content, and therefore no dream work, no defensive function, and presumably no wish fulfillment. It should be noted that Freud's (1920) discussion of these dreams, quite uncharacteristically of Freud's work in general, does not derive from the nuanced study of clinical material and clinical phenomenology from which conclusions are drawn.

Freud's assumptions about the nature of posttraumatic nightmares are tantamount to an implicit model of the posttraumatic nightmare. Those assumptions, shared for the most part by psychoanalytic and nonanalytic thinkers alike, are (1) that the nightmare portrays the essence of what is traumatic about the trauma; (2) that the nightmare has no latent content of any importance, that is to say, that the nightmare is more like an affectively charged memory than a true dream; (3) accordingly, that the manifest content is not a product of transformation of the dream work's serving defensive functions or portraying wishes as fulfilled; (4) therefore, the conflict represented in the nightmare scenario, usually one involving fear of external danger (occasionally with conscious remorse), is the central or only conflict to be addressed in the therapy; and (5) the nightmare is itself part of the stress response reaction, as inflammation is to physical tissue, and is (somehow) driven into existence by the trauma that is represented in the manifest content of the nightmare.

These assumptions, all of them made without supporting evidence, were introduced implicitly into psychoanalytic theory as, in effect, a theory of repetitive posttraumatic nightmares. This implicit theory obviated exploration of the issues of latent content and the defensive function of the dream, attention to instigation of the dream and exploration of the relation of the damaged psyche to the dream. I argue in the pages that follow that all five of the assumptions contributing to the basic implicit model are false.

Having made these assumptions, Freud (1920) postulated a wish to master as originating not in the infantile unconscious but in the ego. The repetition of traumatic scenarios could be understood as resulting from the ego's need to master the experience of being overwhelmed by experiencing the danger with anticipatory anxiety. Freud vacillated over the issue of whether or not the phenomena related to the repetition of traumatic experiences were truly outside of—that is to say, developmentally earlier than—the pleasure principle; he concluded in a later work (Freud, 1933) that they were not.

Psychoanalytic work on nightmares following Freud has, for the most part, not taken up the assumptions that constitute the basic implicit model of posttraumatic nightmare, nor has it pursued the topic of posttraumatic nightmares generally. Ernest Jones's (1951) classic study emphasizes the nightmare sufferer's sexual wishes, experienced concretely as difficulty breathing and pressure on the chest. John Mack's (1965, 1970) work on the nightmares of children and adults emphasizes the roles of infantile helplessness and of aggression in nightmares at various stages of childhood development.

Writing from a Kohutian perspective, Blitz and Greenberg (1984) underscore the narcissistic impact of the traumatic disorders, an emphasis that has much in common with the approach to conflict posed by trauma that is taken here. They do not, however, consider fragmentation experiences and narcissistic conflicts apart from the incidents portrayed in the manifest nightmare. They point to the unintegrated nature of the traumatic scene represented in the night-mare, which presumably portrays, as does a "self-state dream" (Kohut 1977), the state of the overwhelmed and fragmented organism that sees itself as unable to complete meaningful actions because of the disorganization and disintegration resulting from the trauma (Blitz and Greenberg, 1984, p. 107). Blitz and Greenberg explicitly privilege the manifest content: "In effect, the manifest dream is the meaning" (p. 120). They do not take into account the relation of the posttrau-matic nightmare to preexisting narcissistic conflicts, narcissistic con-flicts arising from impairment in the current life and the dreamer, or any of the complexities of dream formation and dream function that constitute a truly psychodynamic approach to the nightmare.

The work of Jones and of Mack does not deal with posttraumatic nightmares. That of Blitz and Greenberg explicitly adopts the five assumptions of the implicit basic model of posttraumatic nightmares just discussed—the model privileging manifest content alone—with which this book takes serious issue.

There is a small but significant body of psychoanalytic and psycho-analytically informed work that deals with the complexity of post-traumatic nightmares as dreams with significant latent content and dream work. The work of Lidz (1946), Moses (1978), and Weiss and Sampson (1988) has already been mentioned. Lidz's and Moses's work takes into account both context and antecedent and coexisting trauma, which bear strongly on the impact of the trauma and the significance of posttraumatic nightmares generally. Weiss's work points to detailed ego operations behind the manifest nightmare.

Wisdom (1950) put forward an ingenious hypothesis to postulate latent content in posttraumatic nightmares that presumably replayed a trauma exactly. That hypothesis concerned bad internal objects, displaced onto the self-representation in the dream and destroyed by the trauma in an attempt to get rid of part of the nightmare sufferer's internal world.

Adams-Sylvan and Sylvan (1990) contribute one of the very few examples of the psychotherapeutic handling of posttraumatic night-mares seen as true dreams and analyzed accordingly.

Milton Kramer (1991; Kramer, Schoen, and Kinney, 1987), a sleep researcher who remains in touch with the complexities of psycho-therapy, takes a psychotherapeutic approach to the dreams of the trauma sufferer that has much in common with the one put forward here. Kramer, along with Charles Fisher (Fisher et al., 1970) and Hartmann (1984) is in the very small group of researchers who are front-rank investigators of the biology of sleep and dreams yet who remain synthetic thinkers in their attempts to preserve the full complexity of the psychological functions of dreams. Kramer's work stresses the importance of predisposing conflict in the nightmare scenario and of current day conflict (especially marital conflict) in the instigation of nightmares.

Working from a cognitive-behavioral perspective, Carrol and Foy (1992) include posttraumatic nightmares with flashbacks and traumatic memories as intrusive ideational symptoms of PTSD: "exposure strategies are employed in the reduction of intrusive memories, flashbacks, and nightmares related to the original traumatic experience[s]" (pp. 55–56). Their treatment strategies, representative of up-to-date cognitive behavioral approaches, center on the use of flooding: "Flooding is described as a procedure whereby an individual can reexperience the painful memories in a safe place where it is permissible for the feared emotional reactions to occur" (pp. 55–56). The technique, however different from those of psychoanalytic psychotherapists, makes substantially the same assumptions as those in the basic implicit model, detailed earlier, that take the manifest content of the nightmare to represent the essence of the trauma.

The work of Freud, of most post-Freudian psychoanalytic dream theorists, and of cognitive-behaviorists (typified by Carrol and Foy) have in common, then, the inexplicit adoption of a model that gives exclusive attention to the events in the nightmare scenario and virtually none to the defensive (screening) function of the nightmare, the instigation of the nightmare, or the relation of the nightmare to a psyche in states of disturbance posed by psychopathology or the posttraumatic state itself. I take up the all-important issue of the posttraumatic state in chapter 11.

The significance of the posttraumatic nightmare as the product of a mental activity to be analyzed is not usually emphasized either by trauma researchers or by sleep researchers. Van der Kolk and his colleagues (1984) regard the posttraumatic nightmare more as a sign of persistent traumatic impact than as a mental product profitably analyzed and understood in the service of treatment. Judith Herman's (1992) important book, *Trauma and Recovery,* a landmark contribution to the understanding of trauma patients, likewise does not stress dream or nightmare analysis in the treatment process.

Sleep researchers have contributed surprisingly little to the understanding of posttraumatic nightmares as true dreams, in part because nightmares are infrequent occurrences in sleep laboratories (Fisher et al., 1970; for an exception, see Kramer et al., 1987) and also because the methodology of sleep research concerns itself with correlation rather than with meaning. Fisher et al. (1970), Kramer (1991; Kramer et al., 1987), and Hartmann (1984), who possess both laboratory and psychoanalytic expertise, are rare synthetic thinkers in a field that, more and more, tends to view dream content and underlying meaning either in simplistic, current day-terms (Hobson, 1988) or entirely as epiphenomena.

III

The larger study from which chapters 2-10 were taken arose out of clinical curiosity in a number of areas. A case in point was a group for adult survivors of childhood trauma, sexual and physical. The group, in which membership changed and to which new patients were introduced, was limited to those who had suffered childhood abuse and who had expressed a wish to deal with topics related to such abuse in the group. The actual agenda of the group, however, was dominated by two apparently extraneous topics that arose time and again. The first topic was nightmares, reported by virtually every patient in the group and the subject of constant complaint and commentary. The second was a tendency of group members, despite the fact that they had chosen to enter a group dealing with child abuse, to drift almost invariably to the topic of combat trauma and their combat experiences in Vietnam.

The problem with nightmares revealed another source of confusion in the clinical literature concerning the topic: despite the use of psychotropic medication that would abolish REM sleep, these nightmares (as is typical of posttraumatic nightmares), persisted or worsened with the use of REM-suppressant medication. In the absence of reliable pharmacologic help, there was nothing left to do but to consider the dreams themselves more closely.

The drift of group focus to combat trauma, rather than childhood abuse, was also illuminating. The choice of topic in the group paralleled the topic of the nightmares at night! Just as these patients by day chose to talk of combat experiences rather than child abuse (the task of the group) or current dysfunction in families (often the task of the hospitalization), at night they dreamed of combat. They maintained the same preference of topic in the family and individual sessions. Their preoccupations and defensive operations seemed of a piece: just as attention to combat took attention away from the more humiliating experience of childhood abuse and the current failure in family functioning, so perhaps did the nightmares screen other traumata in their tragic lives. As the choice of daytime topics might be seen as a wish to avoid the painful experiences of disorganization in childhood and current day trauma, so perhaps the function of the nightmare seemed to transform the experience of fragmentation, disorganization, shame, and narcissistic rage in the day residue into the experience, often heroic, of fear in the nightmare (chapter 5).

These curiosities and hunches led to a systematic study, mostly qualitative in nature, that evolved over a period of seven years, but remained embedded in the intense, inpatient clinical situation throughout. The design was simple. Each newly admitted patient was asked if he or she suffered nightmares. Those who did were invited to participate in the investigation. They were given a questionnaire to complete before an interview of approximately one hour that was based on the questionnaire but that branched out, sometimes in an associative manner. Patients often requested and were given more opportunity to meet if they so desired. The questionnaire began with a request for a description of the patient's most recent nightmare, and then other nightmares, especially repetitive ones. Patients were asked if the nightmares were related to experiences that had actually happened. If the patient said that the nightmare was related to an actual experience and that this experience was traumatic, then that nightmare was designated as posttraumatic, even in the single case of the combat nightmare designated as about an actual experience dreamed by a man who later admitted that he had never been in combat. The dreamers were questioned on details about bodily feelings, sleep, and current and childhood family history. The interviews made use of these items as well as elements of the manifest content of the dream and details of the trauma to return to the manifest content in a somewhat associative fashion. Of the first 40 patients in the study (chapter 2; and chapter 3, written in collaboration with Judith Karger), none of the newly admitted patients who had nightmares refused to participate. Fifteen (37.5%) of these patients had posttraumatic nightmares. The rest of the study was done in clinical and investigative collaboration with Carol R. Bley, who coauthored previously published earlier versions of chapters 4, 6, 7, 9, and 10.

The original questionnaire was expanded to include adolescent and military history and special topics of predictive dreams (chapter 7), delayed onset of nightmares (chapter 6), substance abuse and sleep phobia (chapter 9, written in collaboration with Carol Bley and Howard Fishbein), and attempts to escape from the nightmare (unpublished), together with material concerning diagnosis and medication. It was a striking feature throughout the seven years of the study that all the newly admitted patients who had nightmares wanted very much to talk to us about them. A few said that they wanted to talk, but could not tolerate the upset of reliving the trauma. None refused.

The method employed the dreamers' and the investigators' synthetic ability to relate traumatic elements from the family history that appeared in obvious ways in the dreams. A case in point is of a combat veteran who dreamed of being tortured as a prisoner of war. He had in fact never been captured or tortured as a soldier, but he repeatedly had been tied up and whipped as a child (chapter 2). The investigators' responses were informed not only by the questionnaire material and immediate associations but also by a knowledge of the patient and his or her family issues as they arose in the context of treatment. Our immersion in the details of the life histories, both past and present, of these nightmare sufferers was an essential feature of the study.

<h2 style="text-align:center">IV</h2>

The present work cannot be fully appreciated unless it is understood that the work depends for its strength on the two substantial pillars of a comprehensive clinical embeddedness and of the reliance on a nuanced phenomenology of the nightmare in comparison with the dreamer's discussion of the trauma.

The smaller studies that constitute chapters 2-10 took place not only in the context of encompassing clinical treatment but also in the same location in which the treatment took place. The investigators were also the central clinical and supervisory persons in the treatment program. This situation, combined with the design of the overall study, kept the focus not only on the nightmare experiences but also on the daily and often nightly here-and-now experiences and behavior of the dreamers: what those patients sought out, what they avoided, what they wanted help with, what they fled from. The family-systems emphasis, in turn, broadened the focus to include some of these issues in the light of past familial patterns and reactions to trauma that repeated themselves in current family transactions and in transactions on the ward.

Our awareness of the regulation of narcissistic equilibrium in families—regulation that was often accomplished by frightening, intimidating, controlling, or distancing maneuvers, or by collusive defensive operations that served to defend against narcissistic injury and shame (Lansky, 1992a)—helped greatly in getting a focus on the patient's experience of disorganization and shame and narcissistic rage that was hidden or rationalized by these maneuvers. When shame was not acknowledged, narcissistic rage and symptoms ensued. Awareness of the intimate connection between unacknowledged shame and rage greatly enhanced our appreciation of the nightmare, especially as regards instigation of these dreams by current day experiences of disorganization, shame, and attendant rage.

Although the investigation was psychoanalytically informed, it did not start with presuppositions that derive from psychoanalytic theory. The reader who assumes that the study started out either presuming or attempting to defend the wish-fulfillment hypothesis will seriously misunderstand the nature of the method and the significance of the conclusions. That method begins purely and simply with a phenomenologic comparison: the dreamer's report of the manifest content of the posttraumatic nightmare was compared with the same person's account of the actual trauma, presumably repeated in the dream. The strength of the study lies in the fact that *in virtually every case, the dreamer's account differed significantly from that person's description of the trauma, even though the dreamer often said in advance that the nightmare was simply about the trauma.*

The starting point of these studies, then, is the discrepancy of phenomenology between the account of the nightmare and that of the trauma. It is only at this point that psychoanalytic conceptualizations of latent content dream work and defensive function or screening function enter in. In most cases, the phenomenology of the nightmare experience was significantly different from that of the traumatic experience. In a few cases (chapter 8), a brief episode from the traumatic scene—one with significance in view of the patient's dynamics—was replayed in the dream. In other cases, only certain aspects of the trauma were chosen. There is clear evidence, then— evidence not weaker than that drawn from either quantitative or laboratory studies—that dream work is afoot and that the material in the dream is the result of that dream work, however painful the experience of the dream be, and fashioned by the dream work for a defensive purpose. The strongest pillar of the study is this use of the phenomenologic method.

V

The background to this study would not be complete without some explication of the role of shame in the clinical setting. Most psychoanalytic and psychoanalytically informed investigations of nightmares overlook the role of shame completely, and this omission comes at a cost to an adequate theoretical understanding of the clinical situation.

Freud, for example, emphasized the role of anxiety in reaction to an unconscious wish. Although it is obvious that any explanation of anxiety dreams must offer an account of anxiety, the concept of anxiety as a signal of the danger, for example, of retaliation, does not go far enough. Such a theory of anxiety applied to dreams does not include the wish of the dreamer, who sees himself or herself as inferior, disgraced or damaged, for the restoration of his or her intactness, integrity, or cohesion. The point is perhaps better made using the concept of self-representation (Eisnitz, 1987). The vast majority of posttraumatic nightmares in our sample represent the dreamers as intact, honorable persons, albeit in danger, whereas their experience of self on the day preceding the dream was one of disorganization, disconnectedness, and shame. Thus, the dream work can be seen as restorative of a more prideful self-representation from a humiliated, shame-filled one and accomplishing, in effect, a trans-formation from shame to fear in the dream scenario. This very common dynamic was probably not appreciated earlier because of the lack of nuanced phenomenologic studies of posttraumatic nightmares and because the prospect of being shamed tends to inhibit the emergence of humiliating material in clinical settings and elsewhere, whereas fear and guilt tend to favor the patient's reporting those experiences. Many investigators, like Freud himself, failed to take obvious manifestations of shame in their own clinical material into sufficient account in their theoretical formulations. A careful reading of Freud's (1920) own dreams in *The Interpretation of Dreams* (1900) will convince the reader that most of them were instigated by experiences of shame in the dream day and that these dreams can be seen as attempts to correct those experience of shame (Lansky and Morrison, in press).

Another failure to appreciate the role of shame is inherent in formulations like those of Mack (1965, 1970), which link nightmares to childhood experiences of helplessness, but fail to make the con-nection in adult patients, especially between helplessness and the precipitous and shame-producing loss of poise, personal integrity, and sense of self among others. Helplessness is not experienced by an adult in the same way that it is by a child. For a rape victim, for example, to be faced with sudden fears or bouts of disorganizing anxiety and helplessness is not simply frightening, it is also shaming. Anticipation of such shame often underlies the many constrictions of activity and inhibitions that commonly characterize the silent suffer-ings of rape victims for years after the traumatic event. The fear of loss of poise and personal integrity that ensues when the rape victim faces exposure of the fact that she or he is not like other people is a source of much of the unrecognized and unacknowledged shame that proves a major and often masked factor in the residual trauma of virtually every trauma victim. That shame exerts an often silent influence that may be present for years or even for a lifetime.

The role of shame in symptom formation and in pathologic inhibition came to be appreciated only very recently. This is ironic since shame originally had a prominent place in Freud's writing:

> *[B]y means of my psychical work, I have had to overcome a psychical force in the patients which was opposed to the pathogenic ideas becoming conscious (being remembered).* From these I recognized the universal characteristic of such ideas. They were all of a distressing nature, calculated to arouse the affects of shame, of self-reproach, and a kind of psychical pain and the feeling of being harmed; they were all of a kind that one would prefer not to have experienced, that one would rather forget. From all this, there arose, as it were, automatically the thought of *defense*. . . . The patient's ego had been approached by an idea which proved to be incompatible, which provoked on the part of the ego a rebelling force of which the purpose was defense against this incompatible idea [Breuer and Freud, 1893-95, pp. 268-269].

After the abandonment of the seduction hypothesis, however, and the concomitant elaboration of intrapsychic fantasy, this emphasis waned and shame was relegated to the status of a relatively external and public emotion associated with conflicts over anality and exhibitionism (Freud, 1905). Freud (1914) described the ego ideal as that part of the conscience dealing with aspirations, not with retaliation and prohibitions in the manner of the superego proper. Although a pathway to an appreciation of shame was thereby constructed, Freud did not pursue this trend of thought, and, in fact, frequently (Freud, 1930) confused shame with guilt. After 1923 and his preoccupation with the nature of aggression and the formation of the prohibitive aspects of the superego, he dropped the topic of shame entirely.

Aside from isolated works like those of Piers and Singer (1953), Rangell (1954), and of Erik Erikson (1950) and passing mention in some papers on narcissism, attention to shame was virtually dormant until 1971, a year that saw the publication of Helen Block Lewis's *Shame and Guilt in Neurosis* and Heinz Kohut's *Analysis of the Self*.

Lewis, using sophisticated research techniques, drew attention to the intimate relationship between bypassed or unconscious shame and rage. That connection, firmly established by research methods applied to transcripts of actual therapy sessions, convincingly dem-

onstrates the relationship between anger and antecedent unacknowledged shame. The clinical applicability of these findings is enormous
and of great pertinence to the topics of posttraumatic disorders and
posttraumatic nightmares. For the clinician who is mindful of the
intimate connection between rage and shame, the search for hidden
sources of shame underneath the posttraumatic symptomatology of
manifest rage or withdrawal will usually be fruitful and central to
major therapeutic issues that impede the patient's recovery from
trauma.

Kohut paved the way to an appreciation of the relationship of the
loss of the sense of self or personality cohesion to shame; he focused
on the role of the selfobject in insuring personality cohesion. Fragmentation, loss of the sense of self, of poise, of cohesion of the
personality, is the ubiquitous legacy of those who experience early
childhood trauma; and this legacy, in turn, predisposes future trauma
victims to the most severe posttraumatic reactions. That vulnerability
to fragmentation and the inordinate functional reliance on others
(selfobjects, in Kohut's terms) whose affirming responses buttress the
sense of self are both sources of enormous shame. These issues have
immediate applicability to the problem of instigation of posttraumatic
nightmares. Fragmentation experiences and consequent shame in the
dream day—phenomena that patients acknowledge only with great
difficulty if at all—must be understood to appreciate their role in the
instigation of dreams in general and especially of posttraumatic
nightmares.

These insights have opened the door to an understanding of the
relation of shame and of narcissistic equilibrium in intimate relationships to symptom formation. The loss of personal integrity, the
propensity to disorganization if attachments to significant and supportive objects are threatened or broken, the intense shame arising
from these conflicts, and the relationship of that unacknowledged
shame to rage, violence, and other symptoms have gone a long way
toward explaining otherwise mysterious symptom formation.

The understanding of posttraumatic nightmare sufferers put forward in this book depends in large measure on an increasing appreciation of the role of fragmentation and shame in personality dynamics in general. Dreams and posttraumatic nightmares are
intimately related to disturbances due to fragmentation and shame;
they can be dynamically understood as attempts to respond to a
disruption in the dream day. That is, a dream is instigated by that
disruption and represents an attempt to solve a problem posed by
that disruption. The very disruption that instigates a dream or a
nightmare is also a source of shame so intense that it tends to drive the

whole conflict out of awareness (Levin, 1967). Accordingly, given a patient's usual drift of conversation or patterns of association, shame experiences have to be anticipated and actively investigated if they are to emerge as a significant part of the relevant dream dynamics. These considerations, as we shall see in the chapters to follow, bear mightily on considerations of the function of posttraumatic nightmares—that is, on an appreciation of the screening function of such dreams and of what is screened and why. Further, these chapters shall remedy a common mistake in the dynamic and descriptive literature: I refer to the tendency to dwell on the presumed impact of trauma without taking into account the impaired and vulnerable posttraumatic psyche that, in the wake of the trauma, becomes aware of itself as vulnerable in different ways, dependent in different ways, and always at risk for exposure and shame before others.

The function of dreams can be explored only in the context of the dynamics of conflict and defense against painful awareness that would generate more conflict. It is a central contention of this book that a major reason that the function of posttraumatic dreams has been so poorly understood is that the dynamic conflicts of traumatized persons have been incompletely understood. Those formulations having to do with anxiety or helplessness simply fail to account sufficiently for the role of shame and narcissistic mortification in traumatized persons. The psyche of the traumatized person, especially if predisposed by antecedent or concurrent traumata, undergoes a sense of being broken, unpoised, fragmentation prone, liable to personality disorganization or dissociation following stimuli that do not so affect other persons. Traumatized persons develop an endopsychic perception of their exquisite liability to disorganization, panic, seemingly irrational fears, distrust of the human and nonhuman environment, and lapses into altered states of consciousness. They come to acquire a shameful sense of themselves as no longer being the way other people are, of being exposed as broken and vulnerable to disorganization, without control and without refuge. In short, they are full of shame and the fear of more shame if they are exposed.

What they need from others becomes exaggerated also. Their fears, both of intimacy and of separation, may become so acute and demands on others so great that relationships are strained, replete with shame-rage cycles, or avoided altogether. Indeed, the risk of exposure as deficient is so high and the shame over their fears and needs so great that traumatized persons often go into hiding. Constriction of social activity and withdrawal from involvement are perhaps the most underrecognized symptomatic features of the posttraumatic state. Shame over excessive needs and fears and the propensity to disorganize underlies the isolation of the rape victim who avoids dating or sexual involvement; the rage attacks or self-preoccupation of the combat veteran who feels disorganization followed by shame when spouse and children try to get close to him; of the abusiveness of the abused child grown into adult abuser who turns the tables on humiliating internal objects; or of the often intractable sufferings of the Holocaust survivor whose attachment behaviors or lack of them are continual responses to the irreversible humiliation sustained in the death camps. If the central conflicts of such persons are conceptualized only in terms of anxiety, aggression, and guilt without appreciation of the indwelling and overriding sense of shame, then their deepest inner experiences will be misunderstood as will the defensive functions of their overt symptoms, their withdrawal and inhibitions, and their dreams and nightmares.

VI

The chapters that follow deal largely but not exclusively with posttraumatic nightmares. Chapters 2 through 4 concern the issue of screening; chapters 5 and 6, the problem of instigation; chapters 7, 8, and 9, the relation of nightmare to pathology, and chapters 10 and 11, the issue of treatment. Those chapters, which deviate somewhat from the topic of posttraumatic nightmares are chapter 4 (which considers flashback experience as a screen memory), chapters 7 and 9, which deal with pathologic rather than specifically posttraumatic states, and chapter 10, which deals with one aspect of treatment. Taken together, the clinical studies form a unified whole. It is hoped that they will help the reader to understand better the clinically consequential relationships among trauma, pathology, and dreams.

PART II

SCREENING

CHAPTER 2

The Screening Function
of Posttraumatic
Nightmares

I

Nightmares, especially posttraumatic nightmares, pose major problems for the theory of dreams. If it is presumed that the manifest dream is a virtually unmodified representation of the traumatic event—something like a vivid, affect-laden nighttime memory—then the manifest and latent "content" of the dream would seem to be identical, and there is neither dream work nor the representation of unconscious wishes as fulfilled, nor the need for distortion and disguise that accompanies the expression of unconscious wishes. Furthermore, since nightmares are anxiety dreams which wake the sleeper, the function of dreams as guardians of sleep is not in evidence. Affects in dreams are presumably dampened but certainly not amplified (Freud, 1900, p. 467). Accordingly, the enormity of affect—which has made the word "nightmare" paradigmatic for an overwhelmingly frightful experience in the face of which one is helpless—seems to belie the stimulus-modulating function of dreams.

Perhaps the most perplexing feature of the nightmare revolves around the issue of wish fulfillment. If a dream is the disguised expression of an unconscious wish represented as fulfilled, how is one to account for the generation in dream life of an unmodified replay of an experience of sudden and overwhelming trauma? The dream, in recreating the terrifying experience, seems to act in ways utterly different from that in which stimuli or wishes are represented

23

as fulfilled by the consummatory act of hallucination that we call dreaming.

These issues, of course, have a prominent place in the history of psychoanalysis. Writing of anxiety dreams, Freud (1900) was careful to demonstrate that they were only apparent contradictions of the theory of wish fulfillment. The anxiety, he took great pains to point out, belonged not to the manifest dream scene that appeared to generate them, but rather to the latent dream's thoughts (p. 580), and were reflective of the conflict (either libidinal stasis or, later a signal of danger) between the unconscious wish and the forces of censorship.

But the problem of posttraumatic dreams does not seem explicable in these terms. If the manifest dream is presumed to be an exact replay of the traumatic situation, then there is no evidence of the existence of latent content, unconscious wish, or anxiety stemming from an intrapsychic conflict. The very notion that dreams have the function of keeping the sleeping psyche from being disequilibrated by sleep-threatening stimuli seems not to apply to posttraumatic nightmares.

Freud did pay considerable attention to these phenomena. In the wake of World War I experiences with combat nightmares, and with the evolving of psychoanalytic theory and clinical experience, he postulated in 1920 the compulsion to repeat. This compulsion to repeat can be seen as a wish from the ego, originally overwhelmed, but preparing itself both in dreams and in repetitive acts to replay and eventually to master overwhelming traumatic experience. Posttraumatic dreams, then, were "beyond the pleasure principle," that is, attempts of the once overwhelmed ego at mastery. In these anxiety-laden repetitions, the psyche amplified rather than diminished threats to its equilibrium. In later works, Freud (1933) remained skeptical that traumatic dreams really go beyond the pleasure principle. The subsequent history of psychoanalysis has seen a movement toward considering nightmares through frames of reference that are not exclusively psychoanalytic nor even clinical. The tendency even among psychoanalytic investigators has been to consider nightmares in the light of recent laboratory findings from sleep and dream research (Fisher et al., 1970; Hartmann 1984).

This chapter concerns *chronic* posttraumatic nightmares in an inpatient psychiatric population. The sample, therefore, is limited to patients sufficiently impaired to require at least one, and usually more, psychiatric hospitalizations. The investigation was phenomenologically based, clinically rich, psychoanalytically informed and psychodynamic, but it did not derive from the psychoanalytic, or even from the psychotherapeutic, situation itself.

In the overall study from which this chapter was derived, most posttraumatic nightmares were chronic, having occurred for the most part more than a decade later than the trauma represented in the nightmare scenario. Thus I cannot assume that the sample of nightmares, the chronic ones in particular, are the same phenomena as the type of nightmare that follows shortly after a traumatic event and in persons otherwise free of psychiatric disorder. Because the entire study was drawn from an inpatient psychiatric population, we must caution against generalization of these findings to nightmare sufferers outside the specific type of population and type of nightmare represented in this study.

Posttraumatic nightmares are usually described in the literature, even psychoanalytic literature, as though they were unmodified reproductions of the traumatic scene replayed in exact or almost exact detail. That is also the way the dreamer experiences them. Such dreams appear to have a somewhat different biological substrate from that of nightmares of lifelong nightmare sufferers (Hartmann, 1984). Traumatic nightmares usually occur in NREM sleep, in the middle of the night. Those of lifelong nightmare sufferers occur in REM sleep, more toward morning. Much of the recent literature on nightmares tends to view posttraumatic dreams as markers of stress response, not as products of the imagination, deriving from an excess of stimulation and functioning to keep the psyche in more modulated equilibrium; not as freshly woven ideational product revealing details of the patient's history and psychic disequilibrium and woven from the pattern of personal experience and making use of recent and indifferent materials for the dream collage. That is to say, nightmares tend to be overlooked as true dreams in the psychodynamic sense, having *meaning* not just in relation to trauma but also to the dreamer's entire psychic continuity and having the *function* of modulating excessive disrupting stimuli by representing them in a less disturbing way, as fulfilled wishes.

Most patients in our sample were interviewed one or more decades after the trauma occurred. Accordingly, the study throws limited light (there were only two recently traumatized patients in a sample of 40 nightmare sufferers, 15 of whom had posttraumatic nightmares) on acute posttraumatic nightmares. Such nightmares often, but not always, seem to the dreamer to be simple replays of the traumatic event. Most patients in this sample suffered traumata one to four or more decades before the most recent nightmare about which they were questioned. It has been observed that within a few weeks or months posttraumatic nightmares begin to blend with other dream elements and eventually disappear (Hartmann, 1984). One would

expect that acute posttraumatic nightmares as stress-response imagery would have a relatively short natural history. Nonetheless,
clinical experience, as well as experience in the literature, points to
the chronicity of nightmares. Although there is mention of chronic
nightmares in the literature (van der Kolk, 1984), I could find nothing
to explain the chronicity of these nightmares nor those factors that
would tend to support the continuation of repetitive nightmares
occurring over a period of years, even many decades. Why do some
blend with other dream elements after a few weeks or months and
cease to be nightmares, while others persist for years or even decades?

II

Our interest in nightmares was given impetus by psychotherapeutic
contact with combat veterans and with patients who had suffered
physical or sexual abuse as children. Both of these groups of traumatized patients had a high incidence of chronic nightmares, although,
obviously, the program did not select its admissions on the basis of an
interest in such patients.

The patients were asked about their first and other nightmares.
Patients were asked for their views about the relationship of any of
these nightmares to the experiences of trauma, to childhood experiences, to the current family situation and to the treatment setting. The
investigation also covered details of the current family situation and
the family of origin. These data are certainly not equivalent to an
associative anamnesis, particularly one that takes place in the context
of an ongoing treatment relationship. Nevertheless, an astonishingly
reflective mode of self-inquiry was established rapidly with most
patients, even those whose treatment alliance and observing ego had
seemed minimal or even absent prior to the investigation. This
heightened reflectiveness made possible a limited but significant use
of the associative method and even brief forays into an interpretive
synthesis that was useful to the treatment enterprise. The purely
investigative data were commingled with the knowledge of the
patient's current situation, based on 24-hour ward observation and
data from supervision of meetings with patient and family.

This blend of investigative data, clinical material and results of
intensive family study gave a uniquely rich perspective on infantile
(familial) trauma, on current familial dysfunction, and on specific
current difficulties viewed in the treatment setting and the patient's
current life setting. The comprehensiveness of clinical immersion
provided an unusually detailed understanding of the day residues,
that is, the preconscious preoccupations with which the dreamer

dealt. This perspective was far more detailed than that of any study I have come across in the published literature, the majority having relied on volunteer respondents seen outside of a treatment context (Hersen, 1971; Hartmann, 1984; van der Kolk et al., 1984).

For the purposes of the present investigation of chronic posttraumatic nightmares, I am calling *chronic* any nightmare occurring more than two years after the initial trauma, and *posttraumatic* any nightmare identified by the dreamer as being *about* a traumatic experience that actually happened. Hence, even if, on detailed examination, a dream scenario proved not to be about, say, a battlefield experience, that nightmare was designated "posttraumatic" if the patient identified it as replaying a traumatic event. Fifteen of the 40 nightmare sufferers were posttraumatic under this criterion.

III

These nightmare sufferers had chronic posttraumatic nightmares containing a recognizable traumatic event that had occurred years, usually decades, previously. Most, but not all, of the patients were nonpsychotic. The vast majority of those who were combat veterans with posttraumatic nightmares had volunteered for combat. Virtually every one of the traumatic nightmare sufferers had easily identifiable, gross and continued dysfunction in the families in which they grew up. There was also gross dysfunction in the current familial relationships or alienation from current family or family of origin when the patient was an adult. The latter finding, of course, must be considered in the context of a patient population disturbed enough to require psychiatric hospitalization, usually more than once.

I shall discuss the clinical material with emphasis on the processes of distortion involved (especially secondary revision), global familial dysfunction in these patients throughout the life cycle, chronicity of the nightmares, and the screening function of chronic posttraumatic nightmares.

Secondary Revision

Of particular note is that the nightmares, though described by the dreamers themselves as a reexperiencing of specific traumatic situations—that is, almost as a charged nighttime memory rather than a true dream—were, in this sample, never simple "replays" of upsetting experiences. They were infiltrated with material from childhood or adolescence or with current concerns. They were usually so constructed that the patient was attacked rather than attacking in the dream scene, that is, aggression was projected. In some instances, battlefield scenes were present in the nightmares even though the patient had not been in combat.

That patients *experience* dreams as though they were flashbacks or simple memories of the trauma is noteworthy enough to warrant discussion. Patients would describe as reexperiencings of battlefield situations nightmares that had nothing to do with the battlefield. Some had obvious origins in the early familial situation. Some patients who were never in combat had dreams of battlefield situations. A patient's surprise at the interview, on realizing that these posttraumatic dreams were obviously much more complex products of the imagination, must be seen as an aspect of disguise, a type of *secondary revision* added on to the patient's recollection of his or her experience of the dream for the purpose of keeping the experience from being too troubling and too much a part of the patient's ongoing and disturbing psychic continuity.

Freud (1900) identifies secondary revision as part of the dream work done by preconscious, not unconscious, processes (p. 499). Secondary revision consists of an afterthought or judgment about the dream itself, for example, "It's only a dream" or, in the example here described, "It's a replay of what happened to me". Secondary revision is the line of defense used when distortion by displacement, condensation, and symbol formation fail to dampen the disturbing impact of the dream. Such secondary revision

appears in a dream when the censorship, which is never quite asleep, feels that it has been taken unawares by a dream which has already been allowed through. It is too late to suppress it, and accordingly the censorship uses these words to meet the anxiety or the distressing feeling aroused by it [p. 489].

"Secondary revision" in the topographic theory of 1900 was an early conceptualization of what would later be subsumed under the activities of the ego.

One patient regarded his nightmare as having nothing to do with upsetting experiences in his life.

Case 1

A 36-year-old man stated emphatically during the interview that his nightmares, suffered since adolescence, had nothing to do with upsetting experiences in his life. (Accordingly, by our narrow criteria for posttraumatic nightmares, his nightmares could not be classified as posttraumatic in our study.) He had been admitted for a host of problems, which included spouse and child abuse. Nonetheless, he related a recent nightmare that had an obvious relationship to a traumatic event:

> I went to sleep about 1:00 a.m. I dreamed I went to my front door to answer it. A man blew my head off and then my wife shot him. The man's face was like a blank page. I awakened sweaty with my heart beating fast. I was frightened.

Later in the interview, discussing his military experience, he described a horrifying event that he said had taken place in boot camp.

> A fellow soldier, a homosexual, jumped into bed with me. I grabbed him by the neck and threw him out. I guess he was to be arrested. The next night he came back with a gun to get me. My [best] friend, R, pushed me out of the way. R was killed. We had enlisted together as buddies. I had amnesia for the whole war experience. I didn't even get to his funeral. I still have nightmares about it [18 years later].

The nightmare replayed the trauma in the barracks but with a number of striking modifications. The murder is relived, but this time *the patient, rather than R, is killed.* The dream work deals with his guilt over his friend's death, over the physical abuse of his children, over his homosexuality, and over his longstanding hatred of his parents stemming from his having been abused during childhood. *The attacker had a blank face.* As was the case with his amnesia for events after R's death, he cannot allow himself to be specific concerning the traumatic scenario, which would upset him too much. The dream emphasized that *he is married,* that is, the dream work tries to obviate the issue of homosexuality in the barracks. *His wife kills his attacker.* This element deals in modified form with his reactions to the cruel beatings received from his father and his overly strong attachment to his mother, but also his own guilt feelings for abusing his children, with the fatal act of justice accomplished on himself—as the man with the blank face—at his wife's hand. In the nightmare his propensity for violence is projected: *everyone is violent except himself.*

The patient's insistence that his nightmares had nothing to do with his life experience is a striking example of secondary revision, that is, a conscious afterthought on the dream used to dissociate the dream experience from integration with the entire continuity of his life: his childhood, his military experience, and his current familial difficulties—all of which had to do with uncontrolled and sexualized aggression.

Another patient told himself that his nightmares were "about the war."

Case 2

A 41-year-old man with a history of cocaine abuse and numerous prison sentences reported the following nightmare.

> I was being held prisoner by a bunch of guys, I don't remember who exactly. I was chained to a wall while they prepared instruments of torture. The torture never took place as I realized it was a dream. I tried to escape from the dream and awoke.

He recalled having had the same nightmare around 3:00 a.m. every few months since he returned from Vietnam at the age of 20, He had suffered from nightmares since the age of 12.

His view of the nightmare was that it was a dream of an actual scene of being held prisoner in a prisoner of war camp. He elaborated:

> I'm always in this compound, either put in tiger cages or staked to the ground or carried on a pole with my hands and wrists tied. I got beaten. I always wonder how I could withstand the pain. I awakened yelling.

He had at first attributed the nightmare scenario to his combat experiences but, when questioned, acknowledged that he had never been imprisoned in Vietnam. Questioned about his childhood, he gave an account replete with family strife: alcoholism, abusiveness, and violence by his father. The father would drink himself into a such a fury that the patient would feel terrified if he saw his father's car when he returned home. Father, when in a rage, would beat the patient's mother and all the children. At other times, he would tie the patient and his brother to stakes and whip them mercilessly. At intervals during these beatings, he would take a break and calmly smoke a cigarette before picking up the whip and hitting the boys again. The patient's mother did nothing to protect her children, and the patient realized only in high school that other families were not like his.

As the patient grew aware of the obvious relationship of his nightmares to his early familial experiences, he became profoundly shaken. His cocksure and slick façade collapsed almost immediately, and he was visibly agitated and upset. The day following the interview, claiming that he had an appointment with his parole officer, he requested a brief pass from the ward. He did not return. The next day the ward received a phone call from the parole office informing them that the patient had produced a urine specimen positive for cocaine and was imprisoned immediately. Discussion of his nightmare about his eroticized childhood abuse made it clear that his going A.W.O.L. on the day after the nightmare interview was an acting out in which he engineered an imprisonment, an experience very much like the one in the nightmare. This episode of acting out served to replace his devastating remembrances of childhood abuse with an actual imprisonment.

Dysfunctional Families

Lidz (1946), describing a sample of acute posttraumatic combat soldiers, reported the ubiquity of dysfunctional families, that is, predispositions to traumatic neuroses (see also Moses, 1978) in the histories of his patients. He also noted hatred of the same sex parent and suicidal wishes and observed considerable evidence of dream work in acute nightmares, evidenced, for example, by the patient's wishes to attack portrayed in the dream scenarios as an attack on the patient. Many of our patients reported severe early familial dysfunction (13 of 15, or 86.6%) and upsets contemporaneous with the time at which the trauma occurred, for example, death of a close buddy, "Dear John" letters from a girlfriend (six of six questioned, 100%; see chapter 3. Questions about narcissistic wounding contemporaneous with battlefield trauma were begun after the study was under way. Hence the small proportion of the sample questioned.) These narcissistic wounds contributed to these persons' greater experience of traumatic damage compared with that of others exposed to the same battlefield trauma. Our sample, then, suggested a view of the origin and nature of posttraumatic nightmares similar to that of Lidz (1946), that is, that these nightmare experiences were very much dreams in the true psychodynamic sense.

The following case illustrates traumatic familial dysfunction, past and present, used by the dream work in nightmares involving combat situations.

Case 3

A 44-year-old man experiencing dissociative states in which he cross-dressed had the following nightmare after an angry exchange with his resident physician, who had just set his discharge date.

It was as if somebody was telling me that they were going to get me or kill me if I didn't get them first. Vietnamese, two men and a woman, that I actually killed. Then I woke up and found myself cross-dressed.

Exploration of his early family life revealed a devastating pattern of abuse and traumatization. His mother had brought home numerous lovers and had had intercourse with them in the presence of the patient. He was not able to tell his father about mother's activities until she deserted the family when he was nine years old. He had felt disloyal to the father and unable to approach him. The patient's dissociative episodes in adulthood followed situations in which he might have been expected to feel anger.

In the dream itself, he felt no anger but only the persecutory fear that the Vietnamese might get him. The anger is, of course, implicit in the dream text; he had killed the people who, reembodied in the dream, were seeking vengeance. When he awoke cross-dressed, he felt rage at his doctor for setting a discharge date, and he feared his anger. His current hospitalization provided the first opportunity that he had ever had to feel anger in an environment that he saw as supportive enough to tolerate his emotional turbulence. His acceptance of his own rage in the therapy situation helped him to acknowledge his rage at his mother's sexual escapades, her involving him as a witness, and his traumatic and neglectful upbringing in general. Soon the rage replaced the dissociative episodes during which he cross-dressed, and the anger became available for his work in psychotherapy.

This patient became extremely interested in his inner life following his therapy and the nightmare interviews. A second nightmare interview was held at his request about a month after the first. He reported the following nightmare:

I've gotten sprayed in the shoulder with shrapnel. We'd been evacuated out of a combat area. Vietnam or somewhere. Everybody got on the plane. After we took off, my daughter wasn't on the plane. She was in the nightmare. My wife was there too. So were several (he named three female) staff members. Other nurses. When we got ready to take off, one guy said, "What about these wires?" I said, "Yank them out." Took all of the food out of the house. My daughter was locked out of the house trying to figure out how to get out. I got sprayed by shrapnel—face and parts of the shoulder. Then we were in some kind of a depot. I was taking in dirty linen—pajamas and linen. A short, petite girl had a pair of shower shoes on four sizes too big. More rounds came in on us. My daughter got hit. Then I jumped out of bed.

He said that this was just like a dream the week before. It also involved his daughter. He was able to identify his physical pains in the dreams as actual feelings from shrapnel wounds that he had received. He had several more nightmares in which his daughter was killed.

After an exploration of details in his current life circumstances, it became increasingly clear that after he had left the hospital and gone home there had been a good deal of tension in the family. His 11-year-old daughter, who had had all her mother's attention while the patient was hospitalized, became jealous. He went through a good many episodes of her appealing to her mother, interrupting intercourse, and in general attacking the couple's privacy. Although the patient did not feel conscious anger at this intrusiveness, he (as author of his dreams) included her in the battlefield scenes in the nightmare and killed her in several different nightmares. Discussion of the dream details enabled him to acknowledge his anger at his daughter without confusing that anger with the rage he felt in response to the early familial situation, which had so overwhelmed him.

Chronicity

Some of our data suggested, however tentatively, some explanation of the *chronicity* of these nightmares. If the natural history of posttraumatic nightmares is such that these nightmares usually become diluted with other dream elements and disappear in a matter of weeks to months as true nightmares (Hartmann, 1984), why did these patients' nightmares remain repetitive and chronic for decades?

It is likely that many factors contributed to the chronicity of these nightmares. In an attempt to approach the problem of chronicity, I drew upon the idea of a confluence of determinants other than the specific traumatic event portrayed in the nightmare. By determinants, I mean not only preexisting concurrent and subsequent personality vulnerabilities that may have been traumata in themselves, but also coexisting traumata—usually from early life—that find expression in the dream text (Cases 2–7).

The nightmares seemed clearly to have a screening function for infantile trauma and its residue. Most of these patients were reared in families in which marital strife, violence, and alcoholism were rife. Frequently, patients not only overtly hated their fathers or their mothers' lovers, but attempted to attack or kill that person.

Case 4

A 38-year-old man was admitted, rageful and depressed and claiming that wartime experiences had damaged him and that the government had not taken care of him and compensated him properly for the damage done. He reported several nightmares that were typical of those he had had frequently since 1970, when he was 19.

He described one as follows:

> A fire fight with a Viet Cong. A constant shooting and killing. I was running, falling on my belly, excited and scared of being killed. I woke up throwing up and sweating.

At a later point, describing his family of origin, he recalled beatings by his father that occurred repeatedly and with no protection from his mother, who left the room when father went into a rage. Both parents were alcoholics. As he described these terrifying attacks in his early family, it became clear that he had experienced a virtually identical state of mind then as he had in the recurrent battlefield nightmare. He levied the same charges of being damaged and not cared for by the government as he did at his parents. Although it was clear that the battlefield trauma and the childhood trauma were indeed separate matters, the consciously felt rage at and demand for recompense from the government gave him the opportunity to express concretely his sense of being damaged, frightened, and attacked, and to act on his fulminant sense of entitlement deriving from a sense of early life injury. He felt more convinced that he deserved better treatment from the government than he had felt in childhood about his parents' treatment of him. The nightmares served to concretize his state of mind, the helplessness and terror that were common to his childhood and the battlefield—the latter screening the former.

The same patient reported another recurrent nightmare, variants on a scenario that actually occurred.

> I have an almost constant vision of a man that got killed in my place. He went on a mission I should have gone on. I see a floating head full of bullets or being shot and being blown 15 feet in the air. In another scene he was calling for his mama. With the bullet holes, he looked like Jesus Christ with the crown of thorns. My pain [from a wound sustained at that time] was very evident. I was tough on him. He looked up to me.

The patient reported numerous variations on this nightmare and the feeling of intense guilt that the younger soldier, whom he had disciplined harshly but who had idealized him, had died on a mission on which the patient felt he himself should have been sent.

The sense of guilt and its determinants went back to his (conscious) childhood hatred of both parents, especially his father. In his current family situation, his guilt had a contemporary source that added to his childhood and young adult conflicts. His marriage had collapsed after his wife decided that his self-absorption, rage, and difficulty functioning in the family were intolerable. He became painfully aware that he could not tolerate his children's getting close to him, and he felt, to his horror, that he had become just like his father. The nightmare of the younger man's death and the sacrificial injury and subsequent feelings of guilt screened the sources of this sense of remorse by relocating it to the battlefield 18 years earlier and employing a recollection in which the actual injury done to the younger person was by enemy forces rather than by himself.

In addition to overt hatred of the father, there was terror at the father's violent methods of keeping tenuous control in a strife-ridden household, and also contempt for father's alcoholism and job failures. These factors combined to leave lifelong residua that generated further failures in interpersonal and vocational functioning. The patient's lifelong (conscious) feeling of rage at his father and at his mother's lovers was easily elicited by simple questioning. In addition to the rage, however, was a contempt for his parents and a crushing sense of shame concerning the entire family. At an unconscious level was a shameful sense that the patient had of himself, which resulted not only from his hatred of his parents, but also in large part from his unconscious identification with a man held in contempt (Greenson, 1954). This shameful sense of self, resulting from identification, is only poorly captured by the phrase "low self-esteem."

Case 5

A 43-year-old man recalled the following nightmare experience:

I have trouble knowing what my dreams are because they are multiple dreams. That night it was about my past. I was starting to awaken when the ward nurse checked on me. I woke up feeling very guilty, thinking this dream, like many, was about the fact that I miss a girlfriend that killed herself. I still take a lot of responsibility. The rest of my dream I felt very scared. I felt that I'm asleep, she's either next to me or trying to get in my apartment. It's so real, I'm fully carrying out a conversation with her. At the same time, there's lots of anger. [He notes that a second girlfriend killed herself, too.] She's calling to me. Don't do this to her. I'm leading her on. She was asking me to help her. Why didn't I love her. In the dream, I was with the first one. [He recalled thinking about the losses a lot in the past.]

Curiously, he said that he had called this a nightmare because he wanted to kill himself. The events in the dream scenario actually happened. One girlfriend had committed suicide two years prior to the time of the nightmare, and another, three years before that. In the nightmare, a desperate scene is replayed concerning a girlfriend who subsequently killed herself. It is a small inferential step to assume that the action in the dream, as well as the patient's feelings of guilt and anger, derive from his murderous wishes toward the woman. But the nightmare, with its evident rage and deliberate destructiveness toward the women and his conscious guilt and rage, resonated also with his disruptive and traumatic childhood. He had been born into a chaotic family. His mother was in a psychiatric hospital when he was born. Both parents were alcoholics. His father had beaten his mother repeatedly. His brother and mother had locked the patient in a basement when he was very young, and the brother had molested him sexually. The father punished the patient sadistically with a phone cord and at one time abruptly sent him away to live with relatives in Mexico. The patient had had a sexual liaison with a housekeeper whom he later found out to be his half sister. He had spent some years as a homosexual prostitute. He carried with him conscious fury at both father and mother for the violence and chaos in the home.

Although this man clearly identified his nightmares as concerned with traumatic experiences, he felt that those experiences were the two women's suicides and did not, at first, recognize that the rage and guilt derived from his childhood, nor that the triumphant and sadistic conscious withholding of love was indeed a reversal of what was done to him.

The helplessness and fears of attack on the battlefield have strong resonances with early familial environment. Traumatic dreams screened these early experiences in many ways. Noteworthy among these is the actual staging of the dream setting on the battlefield (Cases 3, 4, 6, 7). While the nightmares *generated* terror—a manifest reaction to the attack—they *modulated* or diminished very powerful affects of shame and rage, very prominent in the patients' legacy from early familial traumata and consciously felt virtually all their lives. The patients not only felt these strong affects but also had continuing problems in life outside of the family with the sequelae of unacknowledged shame (Lewis, 1971, 1987) and rage, either unexpressed or expressed with disastrous consequences in inappropriate places and in ways that made workable vocational and familial adaptation tenuous or unattainable. It seemed as though the sense of shame in these patients derived in large part from their defensive identifications (i.e., identification with the aggressor) with parents of the same sex who were not only the object of their hate but were also objects of contempt (Lansky, 1985) and were a major source of their contempt for themselves. While fear was the major (and even defining) affect in the nightmares, the shame and rage so operative in the patients' waking life are diminished (Cases 1, 2, 3, 4, 5). The setting of the nightmare, then, served the defensive function of revealing the basic childhood fears in a setting in which both unacknowledged shame and uncontrollable rage were neither operative nor problematic. The *justification* of fear and sense of attack provided by the battlefield scenario and the *elimination* of the patients' preoccupations with unacknowledged shame and uncontrolled rage—lived in the immediacy of the dream experience—can be looked at as a compromise formation that reveals fear and conceals shame and rage, and hence as a representation of the unconscious wish to transpose these emotions as fulfilled.

This line of thinking gains support from a number of other findings. First, the vast majority of the posttraumatic nightmare sufferers (10 of 11 questioned) had volunteered for combat. These combat veterans were emphatic about having wanted to serve in combat for personal, not for patriotic, reasons. That is to say, being in the combat situation was their *specific and conscious wish* prior to the experience of combat replayed in the dream. The reappearance of the battlefield scenarios may be assumed to represent *the same constellation of unconscious wishes that determined the conscious choice to volunteer for combat,* that is, the handling of intense shame and uncontrolled rage by removing oneself to the battlefield, where the sources of shame and rage are neutralized or rationalized by the wartime situation. A high percentage of narcissistic wounds, such as buddies dying in battle or "Dear John" letters received from girlfriends, has been pointed out by Lidz (1946) and by Fox (1974), who noted reactions of rage rather than grief in soldiers whose buddies had died in combat. It was also high in our sample (100% of six patients questioned). Such narcissistic wounding is one source of shame and rage. The legacy of early familial trauma is undoubtedly a greater source of shame and rage. Examination of these patients' current familial functioning or lack of it opened up another confirmatory avenue of thinking; that is, that the nightmares also screen shame (often unacknowledged) and rage in current family or other relationships. Alienation from family of origin (13 of 15, 86.6%) or dysfunction in family of procreation (14 of 15, 93.3%) contemporaneous with our investigations was widespread. One patient (Case 4) reported his shame over the fact that he could not tolerate his children's approaching him. Another (Case 3) had a nightmare in which his 11-year-old daughter was killed in a raid.

One patient who had been brutally abused as a child expressed suicidal wishes, first in nightmare, but later quite consciously, and related these to his horror and humiliation over his continual physical abuse of his wife and his children. His suicidal wishes were directly related not only to his guilt about the violence, but also to his shame at having become like his own father, whom he had seen abuse his mother.

Case 6

A man in his late 40s who was admitted for a combination of difficulties, including depression, alcoholism, and spouse and child abuse, reported the following nightmare:

> I was in the Marines, fighting in my hometown. There were gang members. In my dream, I was at my house (in a small town about 100 miles from Los Angeles). Across a big truck line. My adrenalin's really flowing. I'm back where I belong. There was this 17-year-old "baby" who got shot. I laid him on a table. I said, "My wife's a nurse". He was shot in the groin on the right. I blanked out in a nervous state. I felt good. I was back in the military again. I was a platoon sergeant again. I'm important. After seeing this kid get shot, I felt I could have done more. I felt mad. I let him get shot. It could have been prevented.

He went on to discuss his fears in the dream with a sense of shame, as though he were admitting cowardice in a real-life situation. In his account of another dream, in which he was having intercourse with a woman other than his wife, he talked as though he were confessing an actual act of adultery.

The relationship of the dream to this man's traumatic past and upsetting current familial situation was complex. He himself had come from an abusive family in which he was neglected, beaten and deprived. He felt that his mother had wanted to get close to him but his father would not allow that to happen. His mother would have wanted to leave if she could, but she was afraid. In his own family, he ruled tyrannically and by force, orchestrating down to the last detail the conduct of his wife and five children. When he was employed, he worked as a trucker and was frequently away from home.

The dream dealt both with his fear in his original familial situation and his reliving the fear that he had at the age of 17, when he enlisted in military service to escape the drudgery and depression of his adolescent existence for the exhilarations of the battlefield. This man was so unable to acknowledge fear that he felt he had to account for his cowardice when he felt helpless and afraid experiencing the nightmare. He could allow himself to feel fear for someone else's safety. The dream, which took place in his current hometown, also expressed his death wishes toward his children (displaced onto the enemy) and his extreme guilt at being unable to prevent the harm he had done them. To his horror, he had turned out very much like his abusive father. The dream also revealed the wish carried over from adolescence (i.e., with himself as the 17-year-old) to be killed and to make his father upset, sorry, and wishing he had done more.

The nightmare, which he identified as one of many dreams related to upsetting experiences in his life, dealt in a complex way with his unacknowledged anxiety, his overwhelming guilt, and his feeling that he was unworthy to continue living both because of his early hatred of his parents and because of his current abusiveness to his family. The restoration of an exhilarated mood state, easily identified by the patient in the nightmare, had been an important motive for the patient's choosing a combat career in the first place. At the time of the interview, he voiced the wish both to return to the exhilaration of the battlefield—he wished he had the opportunity—and to be killed as a hopeless and unworthy head of his family.

These lifelong difficulties in interpersonal relationships, resulting from overwhelming shame as a legacy of family of origin and pathological identifications with the same-sex parent felt to be con- temptible, *generated further and almost continual psychic trauma in adult life.* Such trauma was further represented by terror and the feeling of helplessness and aloneness under attack and was explained by the battlefield situation and the justification and identity that comes with the combat soldier's role. Thus continuous and recurrent traumata resulted from the interplay of shame and rage in self amplifying spirals (Scheff, 1987). These were evident from the ward observations and studies of current family and provided an almost continual day residue that was a further stimulus for the nightmares.

Screening

The function of the chronic nightmare in screening current familial difficulties was further confirmed by the manner in which these patients described their need for treatment. One patient (Case 4) appeared on the ward, rageful, demanding justice for his war injuries, and claiming that the government was unfair. His threats, demands, and sense of entitlement were put forth with great bluster and self-righteousness. He demanded redress of unfairness and damages done on the battlefield. Only later could he admit that his marriage had failed and that, despite his love for his children, he could not tolerate their approaching him. Even later he recalled the shame and terror he had felt as a boy watching scenes of brutality in which he saw his father beat his mother. That his waking mind split off his battlefield experiences from his familial ones and intensified attention to the former at the expense of the latter again supports the assumption that the dream scenario directs attention from shame and rage in the familial settings past and present, and that the nightmare's placing of the patient back on the battlefield, where (unacknowledged) shame and rage at love objects is replaced by fear, is a representation of a wish as fulfilled. Wish fulfillment is further evidenced if one considers the trauma itself as, in some sense, wished-for punishment arising from guilt that results from rage felt toward family members.

In this sample, then, the chronicity of the nightmare seemed to be the result of overdetermination by a lifetime of traumata. All this could be represented in the nightmare scenario, albeit at the cost of generating overwhelming fear and helplessness. The gain accomplished by the dream work was modulation of pervasive feelings of shame and the rationalizing of the uncontrolled rage resulting from shame that is unacknowledged in the patient's current circumstances. What has the surface appearance of a simple replay of a scene to which intense helpless fear is an appropriate response (that is, an emotionally charged memory, a nighttime flashback to the battlefield) also has the screening function of defensively distorting the continuous and perhaps more painful affective sequelae of infantile and adult traumata in such a way that shame and rage are dampened in an attempt to preserve the equilibrium of the psyche during the regressive relaxation of sleep.

These points are illustrated by the following case example.

Case 7

A 32-year-old man was admitted 12 days after the murder of a friend sitting next to him in a car. The patient gave a somewhat evasive account of his connection with the deceased. He referred to him alternately as "my partner" and "my friend" and described in a confusing way his efforts to locate this man in the weeks preceding the murder. His "partner" was well-to-do but apparently was not regularly employed. The patient had recently been discharged from an alcohol rehabilitation program and was without funds or a place to stay. It seemed to the interviewers not unlikely that this person was a drug seller.

The patient's account of what happened was as follows: he and his friend were in a car going to get a drink when another car pulled up. There were three or four shots. The friend died instantly, slumped toward the patient, who slid down in the seat, opened the door, and ran. The patient. apparently in a fugue state, awoke in a psychiatric hospital, left after a few days, and was readmitted to another hospital.

He said that his nightmares were exact repetitions of the upsetting event and that they had occurred every night since the shooting 12 days previously. He gave two versions.

He was in his friend's car. *A woman came up with a gun and called him by his first name* [a very unusual one]. She shot his friend.

The second version:

He was in the friend's car. There were three or four shots. The friend slumped over. The patient got out of the car and ran [the actual event]. He *stumbled*. He ran and fell. It was dark. He ran off a cliff or onto a body of water. The fear of falling woke him.

He recalled that he had first started having nightmares at 14, just after his baby half-brother had died. At the time when the child was terminally ill, the father, running to telephone the doctor, *stumbled*; the baby was dead by the time the doctor arrived. The patient recalled conscious resentment of the new child, who was the only child of his mother's and stepfather's union and hence (he felt) had supplanted him. He recalled, "I messed up to get attention," especially from his mother. The interviewer asked if he felt that his parents were angry at him. "Yes", he replied, "especially my mother". The interviewer noted that the woman in the dream called him by his first name and shot the other man. The patient added that only his mother calls him by that name. The interviewer noted that in both the recent situation and in the earliest nightmare when he was 14, there was reference to a male more favored than he who had died in his presence, a recollection of someone stumbling and running away. The patient then had recollections of his family: his mother was unfair to him; she blamed him for everything; he had carried around conscious rage at her since the age of four; he resented his half-brother's birth; he was ashamed of his resentment and his neediness; he lived in fear that he would be blamed for those angry feelings; and he was guilty about his anger.

The dream, then, commingles the traumatic situation, the death of his accomplice, with the earlier death of his brother. The latter occurred right at the age when his nightmares began. The dream work, by substituting the mother for the unknown recent assailants, brought his fear into the more predictable family situation. It was his mother's wrath over the feelings about his half brother's death that was to be dealt with rather than the more uncontrollable and incomprehensible shooting of his accomplice.

Despite much dream-work evidence linking the current trauma with the death of his half-sibling at the age of 14, this patient thought that the recent posttraumatic nightmare was an exact repetition of the traumatic scenario.

The screening function of memory that Freud (1899) first described, screen memories, was characterized as memory in which unusual vividness accompanies a surprisingly bland manifest content, the elements of which prove analyzable, much like that of a dream into a latent content that is much more conflict laden and upsetting than is the manifest memory. Freud's paper came near the end of the period when his central focus was on trauma and its reconstruction, so he did not elaborate the concept of screening further. Nonetheless, the concept of screen memories remains a major aspect of psychoanalytic thinking. Glover (1929), citing a case of a traumatic circumcision screened by a hand injury, pointed to the screening function of traumatic memories, which may serve to represent, but also to conceal, even greater traumata,

The following case illustrates the screening of the experience of an emerging psychosis that was contemporaneous with a battlefield experience that was represented in a nightmare.

Case 8

A 33-year-old hospitalized, schizophrenic combat veteran reported the following nightmare at age 20 in combat:

> There were rocket attacks in Cam Rahn Bay. I was asleep. The rocket attacked the base. A room of four people. One got Tom completely out of his boots. Pieces everywhere. Blood. I dream I find his face. In my bed. He's trying to talk to me. [Interviewer asks if he was close to this person.] Yes. All four of us were real close.

This nightmare recurred three or four times monthly for 13 years up to the time of the interview. The actual scene did not occur as represented in the nightmare, but the patient did see people killed with pieces of their faces gone.

He described an uneventful childhood. In the military technical school in 1970, he received a "Dear John" letter from his fiancée, became suicidal, and volunteered for combat with the (conscious) hope of being killed. After several months of combat in which he saw a great deal of surprise attack, killing and dismemberment of close friends, he had an overt psychotic break and was hospitalized and evacuated back to the United States. Nightmares began after his return home.

When the events contemporaneous with his combat experience were explained, it seemed plausible that his recurrent nightmare chronicled and reworked not only his horrifying combat experiences but also—in allegorical fashion—his emerging shattered sense of self and unfolding psychosis.

I am here applying a line of thinking imputing the same screening functions to nightmares as Freud did to vivid memories. Explanation of their screening function may contribute to an understanding of the endurance of chronic posttraumatic nightmares as well as of their affect-regulating function. There were very few acute posttraumatic nightmares in the study. I assume that many acute nightmares may be more like flashbacks or nighttime intrusive memories and that this screening function may have been superimposed on the acute nightmare. Further, these numerous sources of traumata—from earliest family of origin to the time of the inquiry—provided a rich overdetermination for which the original, albeit modified, scenario was a screen. That is, the patient's regarding of the nightmare as though it were an upsetting but basically undistorted memory is in itself an aspect of secondary revision that is part of the dream work, a method of concealing the expression of conflicts resulting from adult and infantile traumata that resonate with the battlefield scenario.

Conclusions from these data should not be overgeneralized. They do not shed light on the problem of how or why certain traumata generate nightmares. The data concern mostly the chronic, not, by and large, the acute, phase of the nightmare's natural history. Caveats regarding the specific sample are worth repeating: the sample is one of chronically psychiatrically impaired inpatients. This is an exceedingly disturbed population that differs greatly from populations used in other studies (Lidz, 1946; Hersen, 1971; Hartmann, 1984; van der Kolk, 1984) and the traumatic scenario usually dated from one to more than four decades prior to the nightmares being studied.

Needless to say, noting the screening functions of the chronic nightmare is not meant to imply that the battlefield situation does not generate severe and lasting trauma. It has been my overall impression that actual exposure to combat, the risk of attack, maiming and killing, having close comrades die, and exercising one's own aggressiveness by deliberate attacks on others (no matter what the justification) exerted a permanent and virtually irreversible effect on these men's psyches. Detailed elaboration of the nature of battlefield trauma extends beyond the scope of this paper. Such experiences were perhaps more damaging in cases where inchoate and unmanageable rage at family members were present prior to the combat experience.

The case material points convincingly to the usefulness of considering chronic posttraumatic nightmares to be dreams in the fullest psychoanalytic sense. Freud (1900) began *The Interpretation of Dreams* with the claim that "every dream reveals itself as a psychical structure which has a meaning, and which can be inserted in an assignable point in the mental activities of waking life" (p. 1). For the patients in our sample, posttraumatic nightmares provided a venue for the reestablishment of a sense of continuity in their lives. Despite the terror, the unpleasantness represented, and the fact that the patients' sleep was disturbed, these nightmares do not require a major revision of our understanding of dreams. Although the task of preserving sleep—a major function of dreams—failed, the specifics of the dream work point clearly to an affect-modulating function. If experiences of shame, isolation, and rage can be thought of as more disturbing than the experiences of attack and comprehensible fear represented in the nightmare, then the dream work, by screening the former experiences by the latter, modulates affect and attempts restoration of psychic equilibrium rather than generating anxiety and promoting disorganization of equilibrium. Patients often awoke with a sense of overwhelming shame and almost uncontrollable rage that became more accessible to amelioration when the dreams were used psychotherapeutically. In some way, the battlefield scenario embodied the patients' wish to be out of their current unmanageable interpersonal circumstances and on the battlefield, where their affective storms, paranoia, rage, and poor sense of their worth among intimates made more sense than in their current families or relationship systems. The presumption of such an unconscious wish gains support from the fact that most of these patients had made the conscious choice to volunteer for the combat situation represented in the nightmare. Many features of the dream work evident in virtually every dream are embodied in the screening function of the nightmare.

CHAPTER 3

Posttraumatic Nightmares and the Family

[with Judith E. Karger]

THE PROBLEM

On the surface, there does not seem to be a connection between trauma and its sequelae, including nightmares, and the family of the patient who has experienced trauma. Such traumata as combat, rape, car accidents, and other skirmishes with near annihilation are usually viewed apart from the family process. Posttraumatic nightmares are usually taken to be "replays" of traumatic events that left the individual close to annihilation, overwhelmed, and helpless.

Where, if at all, does the family system enter? Much of the family therapy and family theory literature has been dominated by those who emphasize the family system and minimize, or even devalue, either the significance of dreams or that of extrafamilial pathogenic "events," including trauma, on patients' dysfunction. Most investigators of nightmares ignore the issue of family (Hersen, 1971; van der Kolk et al., 1984). Even Hartmann (1984), an investigator very attuned to psychotherapeutic and psychoanalytic possibilities in treatment, asserted that familial background was of no real significance for nightmare sufferers. We were able to locate only one report (Lidz, 1946) pointing to family dysfunction as almost ubiquitous in acute posttraumatic (combat) nightmare sufferers.

Here we draw attention to the complex and intimate relationship between chronic posttraumatic nightmares and the family system of the nightmare sufferer. The sample on which this chapter is based was taken from serial admissions to the inpatient psychiatric unit over a six-month period. Most, but not all, of our posttraumatic nightmare sufferers were admitted many years after the occurrence of the trauma represented in the nightmare. Again, our findings cannot be generalized either to nightmare sufferers in general or even to post-traumatic nightmare sufferers who do not have psychiatric disorders of sufficient severity to warrant admission to a psychiatric hospital.

SETTING AND CLINICAL CONTEXT

In a sustained clinical effort to deal with problems of adult patients who in childhood had suffered sexual and physical abuse, we found that many of these survivors of abuse were combat veterans and that a disproportionately high percentage suffered chronic nightmares. Furthermore, it was difficult and painful for these men to keep a focus either on the experience of abuse in their families of origin or on the dysfunction in their current familial situation. It seemed less distressing for them to discuss the battlefield than the family. Their discourse tended to avoid family turbulence and to gravitate toward the focus on the battlefield. At night they had dreams of the same battlefield trauma that they discussed in treatment. This clinical constellation—patients with massive adult trauma and unsolicited complaints of nightmares, massive sustained trauma in family of origin, gross problems in current familial functioning, and major difficulties keeping the treatment focus on the families—suggested to us that a major defensive function was deflecting attention away from decades of familial dysfunction and onto the trauma in waking life as well as in dreams. This clinical picture prompted us to think that the many layers of familial dysfunction were much less separate from the nightmare experience than the literature on nightmares reflects or than the patients themselves were experiencing.

A SYSTEMATIC INVESTIGATION

For a six-month period, every newly admitted patient was questioned about having nightmares. Those who suffered nightmares were asked to cooperate in the study, which involved filling out a questionnaire concerning nightmares and participating in a taped interview of 30 to 60 minutes, recapitulating and expanding on data from the questionnaire. This chapter is devoted only to that portion of the entire group of nightmare sufferers who identified their nightmares as relating to specific traumatic situations that had actually occurred. Patients were asked for details of their current familial functioning; about their family of origin; and, finally, about their late-adolescent and young-adult functioning, immediately prior to and including military service.

In a six-month period, 41 patients were admitted who had nightmares. One left the hospital against advice before we could interview him. All the others cooperated and consented to the taped interviews. The effect of the interviews went far beyond our initial goal of learning more about nightmares. Patients got in touch with aspects of infantile trauma and current familial dysfunction that they had previously been unable to acknowledge, much less to integrate. When we returned from discussion of family to the dream text, it became clear that these nightmares, even those very close in time (12 days) to the trauma represented in them, were seldom simple, unmodified replays of the traumatic event.

What unfolded for both us and the patients was a view of the dreamer as having more complete psychical continuity than had ever before been experienced. Many elements of familial dysfunction, unmanageable states of mind, early fears, wishes for punishment, outlets for rage, rationalizations for terror, punishment for current familial abusiveness—all these found representation on the "stage" of the traumatic dream scene. Although we were convinced that the designated traumatic event (usually, but not always, battlefield trauma) was itself truly devastating, the reenactments of those scenes in the nightmare were more than simple replays. They were true dreams, not intrusive nighttime memories, and the staging of the nightmare scenario served also to screen familial trauma. Such traumata included the patient's helpless fear at witnessing parental violence; suicidal wishes after confrontations with his own aggressiveness; the terror and guilt that seemed to result from the patient's hatred for or even physical attack on the same-sex parent. In addition, the nightmare scenario provided a concrete setting for the expression of basically paranoid states of mind and intense, fearful self-absorption.

We attained an understanding of the patients as psychically continuous persons that aided us in integrating our entire treatment effort. The patients, often at the cost of great pain, were able to use the investigatory experience somewhat as one uses a well-analyzed dream, that is, to reestablish a sense of their psychic continuity (Freud, 1900, p. 1). This enhanced sense of integration proved clinically useful in allowing us to keep the focus on the family, that is, on the sequelae of early familial trauma, and on overwhelming current familial dysfunction, in cases in which emotional cutoff from family of origin and massive dysfunction or alienation from current family were prevalent.

A CONTINUUM OF FAMILIAL STRESSES

Of the 40 patients who participated in the first part of the study, 15 (37.5%) suffered from posttraumatic nightmares. We counted as posttraumatic any nightmare *identified by the patient* as being *about* traumatic experiences that they could specifically identify. We did not include familial trauma unless the patient identified the trauma as replayed in the dream. Only one patient, a woman, identified forced sexual contact with her stepfather in adolescence as a persistent source of nightmares. Of the 15 posttraumatic cases, 11 (73.3%) identified battlefield trauma; 1 (6.7%), sexual attack by her step-father; 1 (6.7%) a recent assault; and 1 (6.7%), a recent experience of seeing a companion shot to death.

Diagnostically, two of our patients (13.3%) were schizophrenic; one, bipolar (6.7%); and the remaining 12 (80%), mixtures of characterological and depressive disorders.

In the vast majority of our patients suffering from posttraumatic nightmares, we found a continuum of familial stress points related to lifelong familial dysfunction. At each of these stress points, the dysfunction constituted a separate and enduring trauma with devastating sequelae. This global familial dysfunction often gained expression in the nightmares. We divided this continuum of stress points, somewhat arbitrarily, into six phases.

1. Early familial dysfunction was found in almost every patient with posttraumatic nightmares (13 of 15, 86.6%). Gross familial dysfunction identified by the patient included violence, alcoholism, sexual abuse, and splits in the family. In most cases (10 of 15, 66.6%) there was overt and conscious hatred of the same-sex parent. In addition to hatred, there was contempt for that parent and evidences of an identification with this parent that gave rise to a crippling sense of shame and a struggle against that identification (Greenson, 1954).

2. There was evidence in many of these patients of adolescent turbulence (5 of 6, 83.3%). This was an area in our investigation of which we had not been cognizant at the beginning of the study, so our data are less complete than they are for the rest of the life history. Often, the patients with postcombat trauma had felt in adolescence that their lives were going nowhere, that they were stuck in difficult familial or vocational situations. They were frequently filled with rage. Most, but not all, of the patients had volunteered not only for military service, but specifically for combat (10 of 11, 90.9%), many with the conscious and explicit wish to kill or to be killed. They were frequently cut off or alienated from their families of origin.

3. Narcissistic wounding coexisting with battlefield trauma was

often present (all six questioned). Other investigators (Lidz, 1946; Hartmann, 1984) have noted that posttraumatic combat sufferers tend to be young and often have had coexisting trauma or narcissistic wounding, such as seeing close buddies killed in combat or receiving rejection letters from girlfriends. Our data confirmed the young age, a high prevalence of buddies being killed, and receipt of "Dear John" letters. Emerging psychosis was clearcut or likely in several posttraumatic combat veterans.

4. The traumatic event itself seemed to be the patients' preferred focus, not just in the dream but in their waking thoughts as well. The patients inclined strongly to talk about the damage done them on the battlefield and not the familial traumas or other dysfunctional areas in their lives. Patients tended to focus on the traumatic events with the presumption that they had been seriously damaged by the traumatic events, but the same patients often had great difficulty specifying how sequelae of these traumata showed up in current family life. The traumatic event then served as a focus for externalization, as well as for expression of a state of mind with a dominant affect, often rageful, paranoid, guilty, or self-exculpating. The patient's discourse, shifting from responsibility for current dysfunctioning onto the trauma, closely mirrored the dream-staging that placed the scene of the patient's upset as though he or she were a passive sufferer of trauma rather than an active part of chaos within the family system.

5. Current familial functioning revealed that in virtually every case (14 of 15, 93.3%) the patient was cut off from or was grossly dysfunctional in his or her family of procreation immediately prior to admission. These data are hard to assess since our sample was limited to newly admitted psychiatric patients, who may be presumed to have been currently dysfunctional.

6. We also noticed, in some patients' attitudes toward the staff, evidence of a split self-representation, identity diffusion (Kernberg, 1984). For example, a patient would present a view of self as damaged, entitled to compensation, deserving of justice, ruined, or chronically suicidal as a result of trauma; but, shortly thereafter, the same patient would become enraged or evasive if the focus was placed on difficulties presumably a result of these traumata in which they were dysfunctional. That is, they wished to dwell on the source to which they attributed their psychic damage but were flooded with fear, shame, or despair when we encouraged them to scrutinize their current familial dysfunction. Dysfunction in the patient's relationship to the hospital staff frequently prompted our investigation of similar dysfunction in current family relationships.

These familial stress points added up in the majority of our nightmare sufferers to a profile of global, lifelong familial dysfunction. While not every patient in our sample was impaired at every stage, the majority were grossly dysfunctional in almost every one of these areas.

There is more than a correlation between the occurrence of nightmares and the presence of familial dysfunction. Our data point to the need to explore the role of predisposing familial factors in the overall and lasting impact of a traumatic situation and the role of such factors in offsetting integrative and reparative mechanisms that might have carried the trauma sufferer at least part way toward self-healing.

Some illustrative cases follow to point to areas of familial dysfunction that find actual expression in the nightmares themselves, considered as true dreams not simply as replays of traumatic events.

Even though the patients at first identified their nightmares as simple repeats of traumatic situations, detailed attention to the dream text and to the trauma actually revealed a far more complex relationship. The dream text and the patient's report of the actual traumatic experience differed significantly in most cases. In virtually every case, a complete grasp of the discrepancy between dream text and described trauma could be attained only by understanding the full spectrum of past familial dysfunction that the patient had suffered and the specific manifestations of current dysfunction in familial interactions.

Many of the nightmares could be understood as the patients' attempt to rework issues from many points along a lifelong continuum of family difficulties.

ILLUSTRATIVE CASES

Case 1

A 38-year-old man, depressed and suicidal, was admitted for his first psychiatric hospitalization after an affair with a coworker was discovered, endangering both his marriage and his job. His wife of 16 years threatened to leave. His three children sided with the wife. His boss, a friend who had previously been a combat buddy in Vietnam, had been so horrified that he told the patient that he doubted the job would be available after his discharge from the hospital. In addition, his best friend had recently committed suicide.

The patient was the second child born to alcoholic parents. His sister was five years older. His mother was chronically suicidal. The parents' marriage had ended in divorce when he was 12, and he was coerced to testify against his father—the parent to whom he felt closest—because of worry that his mother might abandon him or deteriorate into uncontrolled drinking or suicide. His father died when he was 16. After his father's death, he felt responsible for protecting his mother. Toward the end of high school, he felt trapped and enlisted in the military service with the conscious, albeit guilt-ridden, intent of getting away from his mother. He volunteered for combat. When he was 19, he was called home from Vietnam because of his mother's desperate state. She committed suicide while he was home on leave. He returned to combat, sustained a permanent leg injury, and married the nurse who had taken care of him. At the time of his admission, they had been married for 16 years, had sons, age 13 and 9, and a daughter age 12.

The patient felt that before the affair was discovered, his life had been going well. He had job security and a thriving family. His friend had committed suicide after many years of suicidal thoughts and attempts. He had called the patient, desperately asking for help on the night of his suicide, but the patient had refused to see him.

The patient complained of nightmares, which, despite various combinations of psychoactive medication, continued to disturb his sleep every night. He attributed the nightmares entirely to his wartime experiences, despite the fact that he had had no nightmares in the 18 years since he saw combat, until the affair was discovered.

A recent nightmare:

I am walking through the jungle with my dog and I come across a fellow soldier, a friend, who has been hung up on a tree by his wrists and decapitated, with his head being put inside his cut open stomach, with his penis cut off and put in his mouth. I returned to my patrol unit to inform them but they are all gone and I am alone in the burnt-out village.

The patient added as an afterthought: "This is a true experience with the exception that when I went back to my patrol they were there, and we advanced to the village together."

Another recent nightmare:

This starts out in Vietnam in a village. A plane takes me back to the United States. I went to see my father dying of cancer. My father is lying in bed. There are bottles of blood by his bed. My son is giving his blood to my dad. He's all shriveled up and dying. My father's already dead.

The patient's first thoughts about the second nightmare were: "My son is afraid of me. He keeps thinking I'm going to hurt him or something. He thinks I'm going to die."

This patient at first considered his nightmares to be exclusively about his wartime experiences. Only later could he come to see scenes of his family of origin and his current interpersonal situation as being dealt with in the first nightmare: After the discovery of the dead and mutilated comrade, he returned to find his patrol missing. The terror and aloneness after the death of the man related clearly to his feelings of fear for himself and of responsibility for his mother after his father's death—the same feelings that had prompted his enlistment in the military. The dead comrade also represented the friend who had recently committed suicide—a man whom he saw as all too like himself—and, of course, his dead mother. The dream work located him back on the battlefield and in conflict situations in which anger arose, with struggles that were only with males. The dream thus pointed to, but also concealed, the rageful dependency on women that had characterized his past relationship with his mother and his current relationships with his wife, his lover, and his female therapist.

In the second nightmare, the patient's horror at the younger man's dying in the act of giving blood to the already dead older man represented one layer of his feelings of having been bled and depleted by his father, a poor male role model whom he resented bitterly, but also his own harmful effect on his own sons. To his surprise and horror, in his current marital situation his own children sided with their mother against him, just as he had against his own father. As in the first nightmare, the anxiety about death was displaced from himself and his mother onto his son and his father. It is because of father, not mother, that he is called home from Vietnam.

In both dreams, the hostile and anxious dependency on women was displaced into an all-male scenario. The nightmares, however terrifying, kept him away from the painful feeling of being trapped and enraged in dependent relationships with women in which he feared that his own psychic survival and theirs would be endangered if he left.

Only after lengthy, painful family treatment and individual psychotherapy could he begin to relate the nightmares to his familial predicaments, past and present.

Case 2

A 48-year-old man, admitted depressed and suicidal after a long history of failed close relationships and vocational failures, reported the following nightmare:

> One about Vietnam, I shot a guy off a house. He was on patrol. We got ambushed. When he fell, I felt terrible. He kept blinking his eyes. He could not breathe. I shot him, not because I hated him, but because he was suffering. It was my brother that I shot.

First it was a Vietnamese, and then when I looked, it was my brother Roosevelt. I prefer the defusing bomb nightmare over the other one [referring to another nightmare].

Despite the fact that extensive neurological evaluation had failed to disclose a cognitive deficit, this man persisted in attributing his lifelong difficulties in relationships to a head injury sustained in Vietnam. His early upbringing was replete with abandonment and abuses. There was psychosis, violence, public disgrace. His mother was pregnant with him while married to a man other than his father. Both father and mother rejected him. His father was violent toward his mother and him. In addition, his mother was intermittently psychotic, had numerous unconcealed affairs, and beat the patient repeatedly.

In adult life his difficulties were marked. His wife had left him several years previously because of his abusiveness and coldness. The patient, despite being intelligent and reflective, was loathe to attribute his difficulties to anything other than his wartime head injury (although there was little demonstrable residue). The nightmare, however, disturbed him not just because it reawakened his war experiences, but because it pointed so unmistakably to difficulties in his family of origin and to the state of mind that these early experiences had in common with his battlefield experiences.

DISCUSSION

The apparent lack of connection between posttraumatic nightmares and the family system seems the greater because of the lack of overlap in the emphasis, expertise, and methodology in those professionals who treat persons suffering residual effects of trauma, persons willing or wanting to use dreams in their psychotherapeutic work, and persons identifying the family system, past or present, as intimately concerned with their present difficulties in functioning. Indeed, investigators of trauma and nightmares often do not investigate either dreams as such or the family system of the person suffering from nightmares. Those who work with dreams usually do so in the context of long-term therapy (rather than crisis) and individual (rather than family) therapy. They place a decided emphasis on working within an intrapsychic framework, which tends to minimize the need to study external impingement specifically. Those using family-systems approaches tend, of course, to focus on the family system in ways that minimize or ignore dreams or trauma as central features of psychic life or factors that affect peoples' intimate attachments.

The term posttraumatic nightmare suggests that *the trauma*—an encounter with near-annihilation in the face of which the victim was overwhelmed and helpless—is not only a necessary, but a *sufficient,* condition to account for the presence of nightmares. Indeed, in much of the literature, nightmares following traumas are described more like intrusive memories than true dreams, the latter being woven by dream work, containing manifest and latent levels of meaning, involving imaginings of tension reduction (fulfilled wishes) and usually understood on the levels of both manifest and latent meaning, operations of protection that reveal intrapsychic conflict and how it is handled and, above all, as restoring a sense of continuity to psychic life when they are properly understood.

Posttraumatic nightmares are often not seen as true dreams for two reasons; first, if it is assumed that the nightmare is an exact replay of the scene of the trauma, then there is no latent content and hence no dream work that connects latent dream thoughts into the manifest dream. Second, since the generation of anxiety is, in fact, a defining feature of nightmares, then the nightmare itself poses fundamental difficulties for the theory of dreams, which represent struggles in an affect-dampening and tension-reducing way.

In the posttraumatic nightmares of our sample of hospitalized psychiatric inpatients, the discrepancy between the text of the nightmares and the patients' accounts of the traumatic situation points clearly to evidence of both dream work and latent content. We have seen a clear relationship between this latent content and a continuum of lifelong familial stresses, the residue of which continue to be experienced as ongoing trauma. Furthermore, the affect arising from the dream can often be better understood when thought of as deriving both from the manifest content and the familial issues expressed in the latent content.

Once again, conclusions based on this patient sample, an unselected inpatient population, cannot be generalized to include all posttraumatic nightmare sufferers or even all psychiatric inpatients who suffer from posttraumatic nightmares. It remains for fully systematic and controlled research to clarify many of the issues raised: the extent to which posttraumatic nightmares reflect both familial trauma and the effects of events designated by the dreamer as traumatic; comparison of familial factors in patients who have nightmares that follow different types of trauma (combat, rape, auto accident, concentration camp survival); comparison of posttraumatic nightmare sufferers with those who experienced similar traumatic stress without the same sequelae. Nonetheless, our sample was large enough and the results striking enough to allow us to conclude that a strong relationship exists between posttraumatic nightmares and lifelong familial trauma and dysfunction.

CHAPTER 4

Flashback as Screen Memory

[with Carol R. Bley]

A posttraumatic flashback is a perceptual reexperience of a specific traumatic event with an intensity approaching hallucinatory vividness. For example, a combat veteran may react to a stimulus (e.g., a helicopter or a loud noise reminiscent of the battlefield) with an intensity that approaches a reliving of combat experiences. The word *flashback,* then, has the connotation of deep immersion in a relived or revisualized perception that reawakens the impact of a traumatic situation that has not been fully assimilated into the patient's psychic equilibrium (Horowitz, 1969; Burstein, 1985; Behar, 1987).

Posttraumatic flashbacks are often perceived merely as simple derivatives of the impact of an overwhelming trauma. If, for example, the person has been faced with near-annihilation, it may seem plausible to assume that the posttraumatic flashback is, in essence, an affectively laden, intensely revisualized memory of the experience and that the flashback affect is similar to the affect generated by the original traumatic experience—usually terror or panic (Mellman and Davis, 1985). Flashbacks are usually treated as pathological signs, simple checklist items in an inventory of stress responses or posttraumatic reactions, rather than as psychodynamically significant pieces of ideation. Flashbacks are thus assumed to be simple memories rather than psychic activities that are dynamically understandable and potentially usable in the patient's overall treatment.

Several authors have observed that events in some way similar to those in the original traumatic experience may initiate a flashback, yet little has been written on what specifically triggers a flashback memory. Only a few reports touch on the defensive function that might be served by the flashback phenomenon (Horowitz, 1969; Saidel and Babineau, 1976; Grigsby, 1987).

We present the case of a patient whose posttraumatic flashbacks occurred for the first time 18 years after the experience represented in the memory. The patient had no history of drug or alcohol abuse and had had no symptoms of a delayed stress reaction for at least 15 years prior to the first flashback experience. Our observations took place in the context of the sustained investigation of the nightmares of hospitalized patients previously referred to. Our increasing appreciation of the screening function of posttraumatic nightmares set the stage for the conceptualization of this case.

CLINICAL CASE

A 38-year-old married man was hospitalized complaining of vivid recurrent experiences of a wartime memory scene that had occurred 18 years previously. These flashbacks began when he was dismissed from his job, and they continued during the intervening seven and a half months. He had no prior history of psychiatric treatment. He had been married for nine years to a woman some years his senior. He reported solid relationships with his two children and her three, all from previous marriages. He had worked steadily and, before his recent job loss, had never been fired. Nineteen years before his admission, he had been in combat in Vietnam for a year. For the first year or two after the war, he had experienced occasional night terrors; his first wife reported that he had flailed about and cried out in his sleep. He had also experienced mild hyperarousal and some emotional numbness, but no true nightmares. The night terrors, the hyperarousal, and the numbness had remitted completely within a year or two after his combat experience. He disliked identifying himself as a Vietnam veteran and insisted that he did not suffer from a delayed stress reaction. He had never applied for disability compensation. He had no history of alcohol or drug abuse.

The current episode began immediately after the patient lost his job. He had been fired after a period of some months as a trainee for a local police department, apparently with some advance notice that he would soon be terminated. He emphasized that he had never before lost a job. The job loss set off a chain of depressive turbulence, financial strain, and, finally, marital strain. The patient was acutely upset at being fired, and, during the next several months, he began to experience broken sleep, early-morning awakening, diminished concentration, absent libido, depressive mood, and a few dissociative reactions that appeared to be small fugue states in which he did not recall setting out for a destination at which he arrived. The most recent dissociative episode was his trip to the hospital at the time he was admitted.

Almost immediately after losing the job, the patient also began to experience what he called flashbacks—vivid perceptual experiences lasting up to 45 minutes and feeling so real that he seemed virtually to relive various aspects of a specific combat experience. He and another soldier were hidden near a Vietnamese village, having received intelligence reports that 30 Vietcong troops were surrounding the village. (The patient learned later that his intelligence reports had been incorrect. The outlying troops had in fact been friendly forces.) While hidden with his comrade and separated from the other American troops, he witnessed a group of soldiers single out an old villager who had brought a basket of fruit to the American soldiers. They forced the villagers, including (in the patient's imagination) many female relatives, to watch while they stripped the man to the waist, beat him with rifle butts, and eventually bayoneted him to death. The dead body was impaled on the bayonet so that the soldier had to force it off with his foot. The soldiers were laughing, smoking, and in general making sport of their victim. After the bayonet was withdrawn, the leader reached into the dead man's mouth. The patient was later told that the soldier had extracted the gold in the man's teeth so that it could be melted down and inserted over the soldier's own teeth as a trophy.

From the time he lost his job until his hospital admission, the patient had experienced at least one flashback daily, each lasting from 15 to 45 minutes. They were not simply intrusive memories; the patient felt as though he were again in the Vietnamese jungles with the sounds of Vietnamese voices and the distinctive odor known as "the smell of death" to those who had been surrounded by explosions and killing.

He elaborated the account of his being fired. He felt that he had never fit in with his co-workers, and he had been upset by their offhandedness and callousness. His superior, a woman, had made provocative sexual advances and, at one point, had placed her foot in his groin. He reported her to an affirmative action committee. He said that he had been told in advance that he was about to be fired. He was called in early on a Sunday morning by two superiors, who joked, smoked, behaved rudely, and told him that he did not meet standards and would be let go. This meeting took place in front of his co-workers. One of the superiors asked him, in what seemed a condescending manner, if he had any suggestions for improving the training program, then asked the patient to hand over his badge. In retrospect, the light reflecting off the gold badge and the humiliation of being stripped of it triggered memories of the gold fillings being removed by the soldier from the old Vietnamese man in an act of triumphant and sadistic gloating. The patient's flashbacks began at that point.

Discussing his life history, the patient at first related an unconvincingly idealized account of growing up in a large Hispanic family. On further inquiry, he said that his military service followed a high school crisis, after which he dropped out of school. A poor student, he had identified with pachuco adolescents. His father, however, forced him to get a short haircut and denied him the camaraderie of this group and its distinctive dress. As a result, he said, he was taken for Caucasian by a group of black students who were angry because whites had formed a racist gang. The black students accosted him and a fight ensued. Teachers intervened, and all the students were suspended and ordered to bring their parents back with them. The patient said that his father refused to appear because he was unwilling to become involved in racial tensions, and he advised the patient to quit high school and join the Marines. Questioned about his parents' attitude toward the risks of military enlistment in the most intense years of the Vietnam conflict, the patient acted as though the parents (both liberal political activists) were not aware of the dangers posed by military service.

In a subsequent interview, the patient reported a flood of memories of his early years—memories that he felt had been triggered by questions about his parents' encouragement to enlist in the Marines. He recalled that he and his siblings had received merciless beatings from their father, unrestrained and in front of the family. The father was not drunk at these times but was upset by financial hardships. The patient also began to recall—with great discomfort—his anger at his father during his younger years.

Discussion

The patient's flashbacks, dissociative phenomena consisting of the perceptual reliving of an event that had occurred 18 years earlier, followed immediately on the heels of this man's humiliating job loss. His firing and the flashback scenario have enough in common to be considered similar in their focus on a weaker man who is humiliated in front of other people by strong men who have complete control over his fate. The scenes differ enough, however, that the patient's concentrated attention on the flashback experience can be seen as a defensive activity serving to minimize the public humiliation of the job loss and the patient's consequent loss of self-regard in his family.

The flashback experience, then, is a type of screen memory. Freud (1899) developed the concept of screen memory at a time when he was preoccupied with the reconstruction of traumatic events using the patient's associations. Freud discussed one of his own memories that appeared in the course of his self-analysis, a memory that was strikingly vivid yet unusually bland in content. When such a memory is subjected to the psychoanalytic method as a dream would be, it is found to have latent content that is much more disturbing than the "manifest content" of the memory. Thus one memory serves as a disguise for another, more conflictual memory with which the first memory is associatively connected. The screen memory may be of an event earlier than, later than, or contemporaneous with the event it screens. After a few years, Freud turned his theoretical focus away from external trauma toward unconscious fantasy. Glover (1929) pointed out that screen memories need not be bland memories and that the memory of one trauma may screen that of another, earlier or later, the recollection of which is more disturbing. Thus screen memories are not simple recollections, but psychoneurotic ideations serving both expressive and defensive functions.

In the flashback we are discussing here, the patient watched while *someone else* was publicly beaten, humiliated, penetrated, stripped, and eventually killed in front of other villagers, especially women. The patient's own status, and the embodiment of that status in his uniform and military accoutrements—by his own admission, of life-long significance to him—remained intact: It was the old Vietnamese man who was publicly humiliated and murdered. The soldiers mocked, humiliated, and abused the old man, giving justification to and rendering comprehensible the sense of outrage and anger that the patient felt about the treatment surrounding the loss of his job. The old man's gold fillings—not the patient's badge—were taken from the victim with a sense of mocking triumph in the flashback. In the flashback memory, the patient was present as an intact bystander who merely watched while the other person was humiliated. The patient's absorption in the memory of the humiliation and death of the old Vietnamese man therefore was a compromise formation that enabled the patient to express his outrage, anger, and guilt, but that allowed him to experience the public humiliation as belonging to another person. The screen memory served to transform the patient's shame into fear.

The flashback experience also resonated with the patient's initially repressed memories of abuse by his father. Again, the screening transformed shame into fear. The weaker person was publicly abused and humiliated by the stronger, the latter being in control of the outcome. The patient's identification with his father, who was enraged because he was financially overwhelmed, was also evident, as was the suggestion of sadistic and masochistic sexual excitement.

This patient's flashback, therefore, can be seen as a type of screen memory serving both defensive and expressive functions. It is dynamically understandable in relationship to the man's recent memory of the job loss and to his childhood and adolescent memories of beatings. In the flashback scenario, the patient was intact, in uniform, and an onlooker rather than the one who was manipulated and humiliated.

Thus clinical material, however brief and fragmentary, clearly demonstrates the screening function served by a flashback experience that first occurred many years after the original event. In essence, the flashback is a hypercathected screen memory—not the type of bland memory described in Freud's (1899) paper, but an affect-laden one. This memory allowed the patient to experience—with a heightened sense of justification—his outrage, anger, anxiety, and guilt, but to displace his shame and narcissistic mortification onto the victim in the scene he had witnessed in Vietnam.

The particulars of this case clearly indicate that a recent and fulminant narcissistic wound, not a coexisting posttraumatic stress reaction, stimulated the patient's absorption in the horrifying memory. It is worth emphasizing that the manifest conflict in the flashback memory was significantly different from the childhood, adolescent, and adult conflicts that the combat memory screened. In this case, screening invariably transformed shame into fear. This patient did well in psychotherapy, which enabled him to deal with his shame. We believe that therapeutic strategies viewing the disruption as due solely to unassimilated fear of annihilation would systematically fail to bring into focus the narcissistic injury and shame that instigated the screening defense in the first place.

The case material does not, of course, justify generalizations concerning the extent to which flashback memories may serve screening functions. The extended period of time for this patient between the combat experience and the initial flashback cautions against presuming that this clinical situation is comparable to ones in which flashbacks and other repetitive ideations occur soon after the trauma. This patient's capacity to form dissociative states may have resulted from traumas that antedate the combat traumas. Furthermore, the concept of screen memory does not provide a complete explanation of the clinical phenomenology. The screening function of the revisualized combat experience does, however, point convincingly to the need to understand the full clinical complexity of flashbacks without presuming that they are simply intense and unpredictably occurring memories, the appearance of which is only a clinical sign of delayed stress that is fully explainable in terms of the intensity of the trauma portrayed in the memory.

PART III

INSTIGATION

CHAPTER 5

The Transformation of Affect in Posttraumatic Nightmares

The function of posttraumatic nightmares has been of enduring concern for psychoanalytic theory. Beginning with Freud, analytic theorists have traditionally assumed that dreams serve to lower anxiety, modulate disruption, and diminish unpleasure. Yet it is obvious that nightmares generate anxiety. Dreams that repeat traumatic scenes—replays, as it were, of the trauma—prove puzzling for primarily, but not exclusively, economic reasons (i.e., because of the obvious disruption that accompanies them). Freud (1920) held that a wish by the ego for mastery instigated posttraumatic anxiety dreams. But the explanatory force of such a concept is limited. Posttraumatic nightmares seem, on the surface at least, to be utterly different from dreams that prove analyzable as compromise formations, that is, dreams that unfold as an attempt to deal with a disruption, actual or potential, by modulating affect and lowering anxiety. Posttraumatic nightmares, in short, seem inescapably to challenge the notion that dreams function to move the dreamer's psyche from greater to somewhat lesser unpleasure.

This chapter advances a theory of the wish-fulfilling function of posttraumatic anxiety dreams, certain chronic ones at least. It emphasizes the role of shame and of dissociation, both in the formation of the personality predisposed to chronic posttraumatic reactions and also in the instigation of these posttraumatic dreams during the course of the dream day. Because affective disruption constitutes the day residue, particularly disruption due to shame, it has been a heretofore neglected factor in the instigation of posttraumatic nightmares. This line of thinking is intended to be clinically relevant as well as theoretically significant.

The problem of wish fulfillment in posttraumatic nightmares is much more general than might at first blush be imagined by persons who are impatient with or suspicious of theorizing that is not directly linked to clinical application. The problem is not simply the legacy of a theory, formulated abstractly and divorced from clinical immediacy, that presupposes the importance of energetics or drive discharge. Nor is it confined to a clinical or theoretical emphasis on the discovery in dreams of desire, conscious or unconscious, or to repressed infantile wishes as such. The problem is not simply wedded to clinical emphasis or theoretical interest in discharge phenomena. It is metapsychological. Metapsychologically, "wishes" are inferred attempts by the dream work to resolve a disturbance through ideation that serves both to express and to alleviate that disturbance. The dream, of course, is only one example of such ideation. From a metapsychological point of view, any scenario depicting the source of the upset as though it were diminished or significantly altered is a fulfilled wish, even if it is not a conscious or unconscious desire in the usual sense of the word.

Thus closer examination of the wish-fulfillment hypothesis brings into question a central psychoanalytic tenet underlying not only dream theory, but also the concrete clinical situation. Our presumption has been that every dream, no matter what its nature, attempts to deal with current disruptive states that instigate the dream and evoke antecedent conflicts. If one accepts this assumption, then analysis of the dream not only discloses the details of that struggle, but also enlarges the psychic continuity of the dreamer (Freud, 1900, p. 1). The central psychoanalytic tenet put to the test, then, is: Dreams—posttraumatic nightmares included—have a function in relation to the contemporaneous mental life of the dreamer.

My hypothesis concerning posttraumatic nightmares supports the wish-fulfillment hypothesis, both theoretically and clinically, and challenges previous assumptions about the phenomenology of posttraumatic nightmares in the clinical context. Those assumptions concern the nature of the dream (i.e., whether or not the posttraumatic nightmare is a true dream with manifest and latent content and dream work), the source of anxiety, and the nature of the day residue. Central to my argument is an appreciation of the role of shame in the dream day or in the day residue of such patients, as well as in the developmental traumata that color the patient's reaction to the traumatic event. This line of thinking is supported by considerable clinical evidence from the large clinical sample discussed throughout this book. Nonetheless, my interpretation of the role of shame in the generation of posttraumatic nightmares is, of course, a hypothesis rather than a theory.

PREVAILING ASSUMPTIONS

In *The Interpretation of Dreams,* Freud (1900) addressed the issue of anxiety dreams or nightmares as apparent contradictions to the wish-fulfillment hypothesis. Through careful analysis of specific dreams, especially his own, he demonstrated that in the cases in question anxiety derived from the latent, not the manifest, content. Hence the contradiction to the wish-fulfillment hypothesis posed by anxiety dreams is only an apparent one, because it is not the manifest dream scenario that generates the anxiety.

But in the case of posttraumatic anxiety dreams, there appears to be no latent content. Freud (1920) discussed repetitive posttraumatic dreams largely in a theoretical fashion divorced from specific clinical material. His speculations in this work were not based—as they were in *The Interpretation of Dreams*—on his or other clinicians' nuanced clinical investigations, but rather on assumptions about the nature of such posttraumatic nightmares. I am concerned, therefore, not with Freud's reasoning as put forward in Beyond the Pleasure Principle and elsewhere, but rather with his assumptions about the clinical material that were the springboard for that reasoning. I will confine my comments to three assumptions implicit in Freud's work and the implications of these assumptions: (1) that the posttraumatic nightmare is a replay of the traumatic event, (2) that the dream day and day residue play no role in instigating posttraumatic nightmares, and (3) that the dreamer's state of mind reflects the sense of helplessness experienced during the original trauma. I will not address Freud's attempts to resolve the difficulties that depended on these assumptions.

First, Freud assumed that the posttraumatic nightmare is a replay of a traumatic scene, more like an affectively charged memory than a true dream. If the manifest content relives, so to speak, a traumatic event of such magnitude that anxiety is generated simply from the recall of the experience, then it becomes questionable whether the dream can be thought to have any latent content at all, any defensive distortion, or any other alteration imposed by the dream work. Hence this view of posttraumatic nightmares comes perilously close to assuming that they are not true dreams with manifest content woven by the dream work from latent dream thoughts. The posttraumatic state is assumed to be more like an environmentally induced *actual neurosis* (Freud, 1917) without the features of a true psychoneurosis. Despite the presence of dominant ideation (i.e., of the nightmare itself), the traumatic neurosis, with its attendant nightmares, does not seem to be analyzable as a piece of ideation with latent content.

Second, a (usually tacit) assumption denies any hidden trigger contemporaneous with the posttraumatic dream. Freud seems to have disregarded the dream day and the day residue as instigators of posttraumatic nightmares. He saw the day residue as a combination of sensory impressions from which the collage of the manifest dream is fashioned, and of preconscious worries that stimulate the emergence of the unconscious wish instigating the dream. In fact, Freud (1916b, 1933), discussing fixation to trauma, dealt with libidinal fixation only. In this context, he did not see fixation to trauma as a dynamic interplay between a regression from involvement in disturbing or threatening situations, and a conscious preoccupation indicative of the points at which the libido has been fixated. Thus, the usual dialectic between regression and fixation does not seem to apply. Freud did not mention regression from a currently active conflict. He implied that, apart from the particulars of the conflict involved, *the dream itself generates the disruption*—the anxiety in the manifest content. This concept differs from the usual metapsychological stance that *the dream attempts to deal with a disruption*—for example, from an unconscious wish that generates intrapsychic conflict. The presumption that there is no current instigator of the dream amounts to a dismissal of the significance of the events of the dream day or of the day residue in generating the dream.

A third assumption is that the dreamer's state of mind in the nightmare is one of traumatic helplessness and mortification that, because it repeats the sense of helplessness experienced during the traumatic event, is the irreducible bedrock of analytic scrutiny. Thus the dreamer's state of mind is presumed to simply repeat the original feeling of helplessness, but with the added feature of anticipatory anxiety (Freud, 1920, Rangell, 1967).

Authors since Freud have tended either to question the value of the repetition compulsion altogether (Kubie, 1939) or to focus on the nature of repetitive pathological phenomena that require replica formation so they can be modified by the influence of the pleasure principle (Lipin, 1963; Bion, 1977; Cohen, 1980). Referring to repetition compulsion phenomena as "beta elements" Bion (1977) posited "alpha function" in development or in analysis as the ability to process these primitive repetitive phenomena by symbolization and transformation under the influence of the pleasure principle. In a major investigation of the repetition compulsion, Lipin (1963) saw these phenomena not simply as the ego's drive for mastery, but as "maturational drive" derivatives in search of a usable replica formation that enables the ego's working-through processes to support the impetus of normal maturational drives. Cohen (1980) saw trauma as interfering with the linking of drive with experience, and hence with the failure of pleasure principle functioning in repetition compulsion phenomena; these phenomena are clinically distinguishable from behaviors falling under the influence of the pleasure principle. These authors did not address the issue of latent content in repetitive posttraumatic nightmares, nor have authors of systematic nonpsychoanalytic studies of posttraumatic nightmares (Hartmann, 1984; van der Kolk et al., 1984).

Discussing acute posttraumatic nightmares, Lidz (1946) emphasized that predisposing familial trauma contributes to latent content. Wisdom (1949) advanced the ingenious argument that even an exact replay of a traumatic event may have latent content and, therefore, a wish-fulfilling function if the posttraumatic dream presents an internal object that the dreamer wishes were destroyed. Eisnitz (1987), discussing dreams in general, noted that aspects of the self-representation in the manifest dream are related to conflicts currently mobilized in the dreamer's life. This emphasis can be extended to posttraumatic nightmares. Analyzing a posttraumatic combat dream, Adams-Silvan and Silvan (1990) noted the presence of latent content and predisposing infantile conflict.

CLINICAL CASES

I will examine and question Freud's assumptions about posttraumatic nightmares in the light of clinical material. I present material from two cases, each a distillate of several investigative interviews with a recently hospitalized combat veteran. I selected these cases not because they were unique in the sample, but because (1) they clearly show the relationship of dissociation and shame in the day residue and in the developmental and posttraumatic history of the patient to the manifest dream and (2) they illustrate how dissociative experiences and shame combine to form the day residue that triggers the nightmare experience. For the same reasons, the case material is replete with detail about the interpersonal matrix from which dissociative experiences and shame arise. The two illustrative cases are typical of the vast majority of our posttraumatic nightmare sufferers.

Case 1

A 42-year-old man, hospitalized for two weeks, complained of nightmares and of general deterioration in functioning. He recalled that six days prior to his hospital admission, he had suffered a period of intense anguish accompanied by nightmares about his combat experiences, two of which were recurrent.

He described the first nightmare:

I was trying to get up. I had gone with our squad on a sweep in Ah Shan Valley to reinforce platoons. I was a medic. I was sitting there for a month. During a sweep, we were ambushed. Two people were wounded. One of them was a young black man. He got irrational He was worried about his helmet, his rifle, and his jacket. "What'll happen to my gear?" He was struggling to gather his equipment. I grabbed his hand. "You know me. You trust me. I'll take your equipment," I said. I promised that if he would calm down, I'd take responsibility for his equipment. He relaxed. "Hey, Doc, I trust you." So the other medic was able to get a bandage on him. They med-evac'd him out. We continued on the sweep. It provided nothing. Then we went to a predesignated landing zone, picking a point further down. The other company was already lifting off when we got there. The other platoon had three or four helicopters on the ground when we got there. "Waiting up" as we were loading. At a small rice paddy, the ship started taking incoming gunshots. Small weapons were fired. Everybody ran like hell to get to the 'copters. I was like a tail-end Charlie. I'd slowed down in the heat. I was carrying my own equipment and the other person's equipment and my medical bags. I was running. I was 30 to 40 feet from the 'copter. The ground was uneven and I fell. The 'copter started to lift off. Everyone screamed at me. The door gunner was firing. It looked like he was firing at me. I was trying to gather up all the equipment. The 'copter went further up. Then I get this really . . . what hits my mind is, "I'm getting left." That's when I awoke.

The patient said that he had actually had this experience. The helicopter later swung back down and picked him up. He was being left, but people reached out and pulled him into the helicopter.

The patient then described the second nightmare:

I was a medic at the aid station. There was a sweep through the village by Marines. Two ladies brought in a baby 2-3 years old. It was horribly burned. Under the circumstances, we didn't treat

Vietnamese in our clinic, but the doctor took this child in. He had me and another medic debride the burned clothing and skin off the child. Another medic hopped out. The smell and stink— it was horrible. The doctor came in to check the child's ears and eyes. I said, "No." I lifted up the eyelids. The eyes were like white jelly. They were burned out. The smell. I went outside and puked, then came back in and debrided. The doctor wanted to keep the baby all night, but the two Vietnamese women—one was the child's mother—wouldn't agree. At the end of the day, they raised so much hell, even after we explained. They took the baby home. The next day they came back. It was the weirdest thing. They had wrapped the baby in toilet paper and put red gunk all over it. It was their own medicine. The baby was red all over. I began debriding again. Had a hell of a time. I started an IV. The doctor let the two women stay again. I monitored the child. Sometime in the afternoon, it died. Something snapped in me. I didn't want to be in Vietnam, in the Army, or in medicine. I'd seen enough. I kept seeing that kid on the stretcher.

The patient said that this scene had also actually occurred.

He had never had nightmares before his Vietnam experience. He had enlisted at age 17 after dropping out of high school. He wanted to be a medic and had volunteered for service in Vietnam. During his combat experience, he had nightmares in which he prepared for attack. When he left the combat zone, that is, when he was physically safe and preparing to leave the country, he began having these recurrent nightmares related to his work as a medic.

The patient was the eldest of four children. When he was seven, his alcoholic father deserted the family. The patient described his mother as quite distant emotionally. He was reluctant to talk about the emotional climate in their home. At age 12, he had run away from his mother's home to seek out his father, but he then returned. He could not recall details of his state of mind at the time. He seemed unable to gain access to his inner world and his conflict about desertion, isolation, and betrayed reliance on others in times of danger, which were obvious themes in his nightmares.

The patient left military service at age 20, finished high school, married, attended college (where he partied), divorced, married a second time and had a child, then divorced again. His second wife prevented him from seeing their child. About two years before his current admission and five years into his third marriage, his wife left him. They reconciled, but she left again five months later. They started still another reconciliation process. He admitted that he had a drinking problem and an intense fear of closeness. He again experienced an upsurge of turbulence and, 15 months prior to his admission—just when his third wife was planning to move back—he became self-absorbed, began drinking, failed to go to work, and resigned his job (the first time in his adult life that he had not been working), and their marriage collapsed once more. His relationship with his wife had remained rocky. Enraged at the difficulty in gaining readmittance to a treatment program for combat veterans, he became increasingly disorganized, began drinking, and started having nightmares.

During the month preceding the patient's hospital admission, his self-sufficiency totally collapsed. He felt he had lost everything and was unable to perform even basic living functions. For the first time in his adult life, he had lost the ability to see where he was going and to direct his future. He suffered intense shame over his disorganization and his inability to make decisions. He had prided himself on being an individualistic overachiever who was organized and dependable and who earned rapid promotions at work. But when his third wife left, his life collapsed and the repetitive nightmares began.

Over time, however, his first repetitive nightmare changed somewhat. He said, "At the end of the dream, I jumped up in front of the gun and said, 'Fuck it.'" He acknowledged that he had recently felt suicidal but said that his Catholic background would not allow him to commit suicide. Nevertheless, he regarded himself as hopelessly unable to pull himself together, to organize his life, or to start over, and he wished he were dead.

His sense of shame at seeing himself as desperate and needy could not be reduced by his usual defensive emotional remoteness and self-sufficiency. He admitted that his personal relationships had never been good but noted that his career had always gone well. He tended to establish superficial relationships that did not last long, and he found it difficult to get close to people. He recalled that on three or four occasions when he began to get close to his third wife, he had seemed to undergo a personality change. "The nicer she was to me, the meaner I got. I forced her away. I wanted her to dislike me."

The interviewer, in commenting on the manifest content of the helicopter dream, noted the patient's efforts to reach people who were somehow unavailable. The patient responded, "I reach up. I can't get over that line and make a total commitment to people for fear that they'll walk away. I need that helping hand to have a good relationship." He began to cry. "I get so close and then I can't commit."

The patient seemed eager to talk and to link the circumstances of the nightmares to his adult difficulty with closeness. He understood how, in the first dream, he created impediments to the help he needed and consequently lost his own equipment. In the second dream, he was the hopeless baby who was somehow retrieved by its mother but was eventually left inaccessible to help. This man's nightmares revealed, in settings fearful and tragic rather than narcissistically wounding, his desperate need to rely on others in times of danger. In times of stability and composure, his view of himself as needy had been kept from his awareness by self-sufficiency and emotional remoteness, characterological defenses against the shame that his recent dysfunction and neediness had exacerbated.

Case 2

A 41-year-old man who had been married and divorced three times was interviewed about his nightmares a few days after being admitted to the hospital for increasing emotional turbulence. He was a heroin user (on drugs at the time of admission) who had begun experimenting with hard drugs seven years after returning from Vietnam.

He reported a recurrent nightmare that he identified simply as being about his experience in Vietnam:

> I'm going back to Vietnam. I am happy I'm going. Once I get to Vietnam, I ask to go to my outfit. The nightmare begins when I'm back and none of my buddies are there. I'm looking for them there and can't find them. I realize the time has passed. They're not there anymore. I'm stuck in Vietnam. I came to see my buddies. I awake frightened.

Another nightmare occurred three days after he was admitted to the hospital:

> I was in a building trying to buy drugs. I looked everywhere but couldn't seem to find the "connection." As I was beginning to feel desperate, the "connection" showed up. When I saw him and the drugs, I became frightened. I started telling myself I didn't need the drugs anymore. I began to run away. Suddenly, I awoke. It was 2 a.m. For the next 2 hours, I was restless and couldn't sleep. I just tossed and turned.

This patient had frequent nightmares, but fewer when he was on heroin—unless he watched movies about Vietnam. He perceived himself as irreparably altered by battlefield trauma and dominated by the effects of that trauma.

The patient had enlisted in the U.S. Army when he was 18, volunteering for combat. Following his initial combat in Vietnam, he wrote to his first wife, blaming her for his being on the battlefield. He felt that he had been forced to marry her because she was pregnant. After this written reproach, his wife stopped writing him. He said that after the letters stopped, he underwent a major personality change, went into a daze, and was sent home on leave. He found out that his wife had become involved with another man, and they were divorced after only a few months of marriage. The patient is estranged from their child, who is now 21.

The patient recalled that he had undergone another personality change—probably a dissociative episode during which his personality disorganized—following a battle after his return to Vietnam after a leave. He had been in combat near the front lines. Many men were killed. Trucks were being blown up, and he thought his truck would be next, although he felt no fear. The enemy fire stopped just before his truck would have been blown up. During the interview, his thoughts then went to the day after that attack. He said that he had attempted suicide by overdosing on drugs and could not rejoin his platoon because he was too drowsy after the overdose. He refused to do KP, and he physically attacked a captain. A sergeant asked him to return to his old platoon, but he replied, "I can't. I'm scared. I can't be in the point truck." (The man who had taken that position was burned to death when a gasoline can exploded.) He refused to sign an Article 15 (a written reprimand) and was finally court-martialed. To the interviewer he said, "I failed in my duty." The interviewer interjected that anybody would be scared under those circumstances. The patient replied, "Yeah, after the first attack, the lieutenant was in shock. Two sergeants ran away. I grew up religious, though. So I wasn't afraid [at the time]." His rage and sense of devastation seemed more centered on his recollection that the survivors had completely lost their composure and fled than it was on the widespread killing or danger to himself during the day in combat.

He claimed that he had felt no fear in Vietnam except during the first weeks when he saw combat troops engaged in such brutalities as collecting the ears of dead Vietcong soldiers. He recalled an enemy soldier having his jaw shot off and another one with his penis shot. After the big battle, he kept away from everyone. His personality again disorganized and he underwent a change. He said that he had never been the same since his combat experience.

The patient described, a deterioration of composure, morale, self-respect, and bodily and emotional integrity in his outfit and in himself that reminded him of his early upbringing. The second of four children, he had grown up in a home with his mother and stepfather. His father had deserted the family when the patient was quite young. His mother was close to the two youngest of the four children, but not to the patient or his older sister. He remembered his mother as enslaved by work, or sick in some undefinable way. She frequently remained in bed, upset and dysfunctional. She often flew into a rage and beat him and urged him to drop out of school to support the family. He did quit school, but avoided being the family breadwinner, although he felt now that he should have taken on that responsibility. Suddenly tearful, he recalled that he had been abused at age 12 or 13 by a stranger who pulled his pants down and penetrated him anally. He ran away, bleeding, went to a movie, cleaned himself off, and told nobody about the assault until he told his ward therapist following admission.

He said offhandedly that he had had lots of sex early in life with both men and women. A male baby-sitter apparently had abused him when he was about three years old. He also recalled being left with a sitter, a woman of about 25, who took him to bed and had him fondle her.

Asked if he had felt fear in connection with these early sexual activities, he replied, "No, I felt betrayed." Then he revealed, "My mom would beat me." Later, showing cognizance of his tendency to deny fear, he explained, "When I get scared, I go forward, like I did in Vietnam. Then I felt fear about the abuse at age 13, not about combat. I was filled with shame. I felt people could look at me and know. I was paranoid all the time, as though people could tell what had happened to me."

The patient became distraught, and his thoughts shifted from his mother to his second wife. He gave a somewhat inconsistent account of his second marriage, which lasted 11 or 12 years and had been, in his opinion, a mistake. "I felt ashamed. I felt like a woman. I felt all the shame from the abuse. She was getting close to me. How do I hide it? It was my torment." His thoughts again shifted to his childhood: "I felt that the abuse at 13 took my manhood away. It left me feeling like a sissy. That's why I withdrew and used heroin."

Looking at his life in retrospect, he identified four situations—major dissociative episodes, perhaps—when his personality changed: the sexual abuse at age 13, the return home to divorce his first wife, the aftermath of the big battle in Vietnam, and the trip home from Vietnam during which his fear emerged. He had been frightened ever since.

The relationship of his drug use to his chaotic state of mind became clearer: "I got to the point where I was using drugs. I was arrested for heroin. My life was going nowhere. I couldn't face anybody anymore. I felt withdrawn even when awake. The only people in my life were my connection and the people I'd fix drugs with." As the patient's narrative progressed, the mixture of dissociative episodes and his shame and craving for heroin to ablate his shameful consciousness in the two or three days preceding the nightmare became more evident.

Returning to the second nightmare, the interviewer noted that it was about a "connection" and that the patient had used heroin to forget both the war and the memories of sexual abuse. The patient replied, "Yes. I recall something. In the poolroom on the ward, on the day after the nightmare, I felt full of shame. All those feelings came back, like when I was abused." The interviewer inquired about the relationship between the patient's use of heroin and those feelings of shame. "Yeah, heroin got me out of it. I felt a lot of shame. I felt dirty. I felt like a female, real weak. Sometimes my shame gets so bad, I feel like a woman. Someone's going to rape me again. I withdraw." The interviewer added, "And use drugs?" "Only heroin," the patient said. "I still carry the feeling. That's why I can't get close to people. I don't know how to get rid of it."

The patient's current state of mind was most evident when he talked about his third marriage, which had involved numerous fights, both physical and verbal. Not only had he hit his wife, but she had also struck him. He commented: "I have not seen her since September. We were married five months." He then described his paranoid state of mind:

> "I thought she wanted sex with everyone. I wanted her to have sex with men while I watched, yet I was jealous. We were together 8 months. I left. Then I went back to the house to see if she was with someone. She was, and I haven't seen her since. That was in September. I'd reconcile, only if she was faithful. She probably wouldn't agree. She loved me. She said, crying, 'You're draining me emotionally. You put walls up.' I would want a reconciliation. I treated her so bad. I had been in touch with her by phone. She doesn't know I'm in the hospital. Nobody does."

Asked if he kept his hospitalization secret because he did not want to be seen as a failure, he replied, "Yeah, it's humiliating. I don't want to be seen as a failure again. I tried 50 or 60 times to get off drugs. My family always wonder. I've come a long way. I was literally insane after Vietnam. Now I'm articulate, but my mind's not here."

All this material was the day residue, the affective tone of the dream day accompanied by dissociative experiences and the patient's shameful view of himself that preceded the nightmares. Both night-mares can be seen as responses to, and attempts to deal with, the personality disorganization that had unfolded prior to his hospitaliza-tion. In the first dream, his wish to unite with the outfit gave him a sense of integrity, masculine identity, and belonging in a context in which danger was only from without rather than from shameful collapse within himself (the day residue) or his outfit (his recollection of the disorganization after the battle). In the second dream, the wish to annihilate his state of mind with drugs became terrifying when it conferred on him the identity of a drug user, and hence a failure and an outcast in the eyes of his family. He had struggled against this identity for years.

ASSUMPTIONS IN THE LIGHT OF CLINICAL MATERIAL

These clinical cases illustrate the matrix of dissociation and shame, especially during the dream day. They support my reconsideration of the assumptions I discussed earlier: that the dream has no latent content, that the anxiety arises from the same conflict as does the danger in the manifest content, and that the day residue is not a significant instigator of the dream. These patients' dreams should not be seen simply as replays of traumatic situations, the impact of which may be presumed to be obvious (i.e., that a relatively intact psyche is somehow acted on by a disturbing memory). In Case 1, the dreamer's (i.e., the dream work's) choice of these (presumably actual) scenes was overdetermined by his history, as evidenced by his associations at the time of the interview. The patient's associations were related to abandonment and hopelessness and to the consequent obstacles to close relationships. In Case 2, the patient's description of the battle-field trauma does not at all match the story in the dream scenario. Both patients confidently described their dreams—at least before being questioned—as simply about wartime experiences.

In neither case is the emotional state in the dreams an uncompli-cated instance of infantile helplessness in its most basic form. In Case 1, the dreams concern trying to rejoin significant helping others in a situation of danger despite obstacles to that rapprochement. In this man's second nightmare (the baby in red), the patient displaces, with horror but without shame, his sense of himself as fundamentally hopeless, infantile, beyond repair, and mistreated by his nurturers. In Case 2, the anxiety that awakened the patient was not at all like the narcissistic rage and shame that he had felt in combat. The dream transformed the experience of narcissistic wounding (when he com-prehended the damage done to his platoon) into separation anxiety by the staging of the dream scenario onto the battlefield. In both cases, the dreams can be seen as dealing with anxieties derived from early familial trauma in which the patient had been humbled and shamed and that aroused intense castration anxiety. In Case 2, there is also a coexisting narcissistic wound—loss of integrity and desertion after combat by members of the patient's outfit.

It is also clear that both patients had experienced overwhelming disturbance in the dream day, disturbance that constituted the day residue instigating the dream and to which the dream was a response. In each case, the nightmare attempted to transform shame from the dream day into some other affect experienced in the context of the battlefield scene. These considerations are masked, of course, by part of the dream work that caused the dream to be considered something remote, alien, and disconnected from current-day experiences, that is, the secondary revision (Freud, 1900)—the patient's conscious experience in his statement about the dream. Thus the conscious belief, "It's about what happened in Vietnam," represents another layer of defense against painful awareness. In each instance, the patient experienced enormous relief in talking about the dreams and wanted to talk more. Once each patient acknowledged his feeling of shame at his battlefield performance, his thoughts focused on the earlier shame in his life; and, even though these thoughts upset him, he experienced a sense of continuity and relief, although clearly not total amelioration of the disruptive posttraumatic state.

My hypothesis that posttraumatic nightmares transform shame into other affects depends on the finding, in these cases and in many others, that *the basic traumatic state in the latent dream thoughts that triggers the nightmare is distinctly different from the state of helplessness portrayed in the manifest dream, in which the traumatized person is overwhelmed by danger before anticipatory anxiety can be experienced.* The latter situation is what Freud (1920) assumed in *Beyond the Pleasure Principle* (see Rangell, 1967). The basic traumatic state in these patients (and in most others in the study) has to do with narcissistic mortification in the presence of other people. In predisposing traumatic situations in childhood, the first patient's feeling of being neglected or deserted in time of danger, his sense of hopeless defectiveness, and his placing obstacles in the pathway of bonding to others all derive from his upbringing and remain enduring sources of shame. The second patient's vulnerable psyche became traumatized and humiliated in the context of intense dependency on the humiliator, his mother, and on the man who raped him—so much so that exposure, closeness, and dependency itself are seen by the patient as humiliating. He had viewed himself since childhood as mortified, distressed, and humbled before his mother, the very person on whom he desperately depended.

Childhood narcissistic wounding is further compounded by coexisting narcissistic wounds if, for example, a combat soldier has seen buddies die or has received a "Dear John" letter (Lidz, 1946). In the second patient's nightmare scenario, the narcissistic wound of witnessing the destruction of the morale, poise, and courage of his platoon is transformed into a simpler separation anxiety without narcissistic wounding.

The sequelae of these traumata—fear, self-absorption, preoccupation, inability to tolerate other people's needs, emotional blunting, and dissociative states—are also sources of interpersonal failure and hence of shame, especially because they occurred in contexts in which the shame was not acknowledged. In the first case, the patient's narcissistic equilibrium collapsed after his third marriage ended because of his alcoholism and destructive rage at the time of attempted reconciliation. The situation is, of course, more complicated if it is, as in the second case, compounded by paranoid, homosexual, or masochistic fantasies that themselves generate shame. The type of shame experienced by the second patient, accompanied by dissociative states or fragmentation experiences, constituted for him a reliving of humiliating experiences from childhood. The sadistic beatings, the homosexual rape, and the dissolution of integrity in his platoon fostered the traumatic event in the dream. For the first patient, the traumatic state revived the humiliation of not seeing himself as self-sufficient. The trauma of both dreamers is further complicated by their shame at having failed at significant aspects of interpersonal relationships—that is, relating well to love objects, attending to others' needs, and conducting life the way others do, free of malignant affect and panic-laden constriction in the face of what seem to be ordinary activities.

It is here that the metapsychologically economic question of why fear is preferable to shame may be considered. The childhood trauma and the conflicts in the day residue of both these patients (and in the vast majority of those in our sample) reveal that shame is the affect attendant on seeing oneself in the eyes of others as not merely in danger, but as incohesive, inadequate, unlovable, and incapable of taking steps that would restore a sense of worth to the dreamer. In the dreams, however, the self-representation (Eisnitz, 1987) has become that of one exposed to external danger. The nightmare scenario, then, transforms narcissistic mortification and inescapable unacceptability

accompanied by shame into external danger (or, in Case 2, temptation) accompanied by fear that befalls an otherwise acceptable person. (The role of guilt is taken up in chapter 11.)

THE TRANSFORMATION OF SHAME INTO FEAR

In the light of the foregoing considerations, I will attempt a tentative
reconstruction of the larger context for the formation of some types
of posttraumatic dreams, both acute and chronic. The clinical material does not point inevitably to my conclusions, but the case studies
should enable the reader to follow my rationale.

My hypothesis involves a sequence of five events: (1) the antecedent or predisposing trauma in childhood, (2) the trauma itself and
its contemporaneous events, (3) the chronic posttraumatic state,
(4) the events of the dream day, and (5) the dream formation.

First, childhood trauma predisposes the patient to dissociation,
lack of cohesion in the personality, and a sense of shame that endures
and recurs during states of diminished cohesion (Moses, 1978). The
first patient's running away from home suggests a degree of trauma
more intense than was indicated by his narrative. The second patient's beatings and homosexual rape are more concrete episodes in a
childhood replete with recurrent and humiliating trauma.

Second, events contemporaneous with the trauma are repeated in
the dream. The traumatic event, frequently an aspect of the event
portrayed in the dream, is not in itself shameful or humiliating. None
of the combat dreams were humiliating. Many such patients do not
experience the actual situation in the posttraumatic dream as shameful. The trauma itself, especially if it is accompanied by a deliberate
intent to humble or humiliate or degrade, may be narcissistically
wounding (e.g., with rape victims, mugging victims, or Holocaust
survivors), but the scene replayed usually is not so. In Case 1, the
"helicopter" dream screened the patient's sense of failure at de-
stroying relationships and the "red baby" dream displaced hopelessness and inadequate nurturance onto the ill-fated infant. The loss of
the integrity of his platoon was, for the second patient, such a
narcissistic wound (Fox, 1974).

It should be noted that in these two cases, each patient had chosen
to enter a situation in which trauma became not only likely but also
virtually inevitable. The adolescent wish to replace shame (at life
failures) with fear of attack (on the battlefield) parallels the wish in the
latent dream thoughts.

There may be coexisting narcissistic wounding, especially in
younger persons in combat, for example, when a close buddy dies or

the soldier receives a "Dear John" letter. The second patient's marital difficulties, which caused his wife to stop writing to him, constituted such a narcissistic wound.

Third, the chronic posttraumatic state leaves the patient vulnerable to anxiety, preoccupation, and dissociative states. The proclivity to enter this state of mind itself becomes a narcissistic wound: These traumatized patients are not like other people; they cannot do what other people can do; they often cannot tolerate other people; and they have an excessive fear of surroundings that constantly threaten them with exposure and shame if they act as other people do. Often the posttraumatic state is interpreted on the basis of the antecedent trauma. The commonly observed clinical result is the constriction of activity or avoidance of intimacy so commonly found in traumatized persons. The global marital difficulties of the two patients illustrate this point.

Fourth, events in the dream day constitute the day residue for the posttraumatic dream. These events may (and often are) ongoing in the day-to-day experience of persons with repetitive posttraumatic dreams. In the dream day, posttraumatic vulnerability is intensified by a narcissistic wound (or many wounds) resulting from some interpersonal failure such as an inability to become emotionally involved or a dissociative episode. *It is from awareness of these interpersonal failures that shame arises as a signal that the patient is cut off from the possibility of meaningful bonding. These patients thus perceive themselves as different from other people and outside of, as well as unworthy of, meaningful attachments.*

Unconscious fantasy links this fragmented or dissociated state to the predisposing trauma, with a corresponding dramatic increase in shame. The first patient's unconscious link to predisposing trauma is evident from his associations to the nightmare. The second patient said that after a conflict on the ward he felt vulnerable, fragmented, "like a woman."

The fifth, and final, event in the sequence is the operation of dream formation itself. The crux of my hypothesis is the assumption that the increase in shame instigates a wish that is accompanied by the reexperiencing of some aspect of the traumatic event. It is a wish because it allows for a decrease in disruption due to shame. This activity of the dream work constitutes a trade-off of states of mind— shame is transformed into fear—and of stances—shameful aspects of the self-representation are transformed into fearful ones. Preoccupation with the traumatic event is already a facilitated pathway; that is, the absorption in the memory of some aspect of the traumatic event defends against the experience of mortification and narcissistic wounding in the dream day. This phenomenon is more apparent if, as in both the present cases, there is some connection between conscious choice and the trauma: the patients chose to enlist in combat as a resolution of essentially the same struggle in adolescence. This *saturation of the current shameful and fragmented state into the wish* (to return to the battlefield) is an incomplete trade-off.

The wish for the aspect of self-representation revealed in the traumatic event results in drastically increased castration anxiety and persecutory anxiety. Residual shame (which is unacknowledged because such acknowledgment would generate more shame) results in narcissistic rage. (I am assuming that the transformation of shame into narcissistic rage is a general property of unacknowledged shame [Lewis, 1971].) This rage is then projected by the dream work and is experienced as persecutory anxiety—hence the dramatic increase in anxiety that may be accounted for by the scenario in the manifest content of the dream. The nightmare is an attempt (by definition a somewhat ineffective one) to deal with the disturbance. That is, *the dream work is trying to do something about the awareness of dissociation and shame that constitutes the day residue*. However disturbing the scenario may be, a wish is fulfilled. The dreamer's self-representation (Eisnitz, 1987) has changed from that of one who has been found unacceptable to that of one who is in danger. The dreamer has become like other people, reacting to external danger the same way that anyone else would. On the dream day, secondary revision—a preconscious part of the dream work that further defends against shame—seals the dream off from its association with narcissistic wounding by the pronouncement, "It is a dream about the trauma," or "I dreamed about the trauma in the war."

DISCUSSION

This view of posttraumatic nightmares has far-reaching implications, both theoretical and clinical. The elements of dream formation portray dominant ideation that serves as a compromise formation by shifting attention from one trauma (or at least the aspect that is not accompanied by shame) to another trauma. This compromise formation can screen numerous other forms of traumata, including infantile trauma, trauma coexisting with the traumatic scene, and trauma contemporaneous with the dream in which shame is a major component. The posttraumatic nightmare, however disturbing, screens out experiences of shame, often from a lifetime of traumata (see chapter 2).

The dream, therefore, despite the overt discomfort that it seems to generate, is attempting to minimize the experience of shame by changing circumstances and by transforming it into rage and consequent anxiety or fear of attack. (The role of guilt that results from such rage is discussed in chapter 11.) The attempt is to modulate the disturbance caused by shame in the contemporaneous narcissistic wounding in the dream day. If this motivating force is not appreciated, psychoanalytic understanding is incomplete both clinically and theoretically.

Thus posttraumatic nightmares, at least the preponderance of them in the present sample, are true dreams, not simply relived memories in which the dreamer's psyche has been impinged on by the recollection of traumatic events. The clinical picture is similar to that of a true psychoneurosis, one superimposed on a repetitively traumatized psyche since it is dominated by a pathological idea that diverts attention from an even more upsetting latent idea, as is the case with obsessions, phobias, and conversions. In this instance, the "idea" is the manifest nightmare, the analysis of which proceeds *pari passu* with the handling of the resistance that is aimed at reducing shame. The latent content is to be found in the fragmentation and shame in the dream day that instigates the nightmare.

Posttraumatic nightmares of the type I have described, like psychoneurotic symptoms, are active products of psychic construction by the dream work, not passive replays of traumatic occurrences somehow controlled by the memory of a past event that impinges on a passive psyche. I cannot emphasize too strongly that *the conflict in the latent dream thought is not the same as the conflict represented in the manifest content of the dream*. It is the conflict in the latent thought, not that in the manifest content, that instigates the dream. Accordingly, interpretations or interventions predicated on the assumption that the "obvious" conflict in the manifest content is central in the current clinical picture ignore the predisposing trauma (which is replete with humiliation and vulnerability in personality organization), the posttraumatic vulnerability and its consequent narcissistic wounding, and the highly conflictual matrix of shame and dissociation in the dream day. Any therapeutic approach involving naive empathy or simple abreaction based solely on the scenario in the manifest content, insofar as it presumes that there is no latent content, is at best incomplete and inexact and at worst a countertransference collusion that produces a therapeutic bypass of conflict involving shame, dissociation, and rage. That this conflict centers on experiences of shame and itself poses further risk of exposure and more shame perhaps explains why it has escaped detection and theoretical attention for so long. Only when the shame is explored and acknowledged does the psychotherapeutic process succeed in ameliorating the psychoneurotic aspect of the posttraumatic reaction.

This last point is supported by considering how the exploration of these nightmares has been used in the treatment of nonpsychotic patients (see chapters 4 and 10). It is noteworthy that these patients, although often reluctant at first, wanted to talk about their dreams, explore them, and reflect on their relationship to the present and the past. Nonpsychotic nightmare sufferers invariably had a great deal of narcissistic injury in their developmental history, shame conflict coexisting with, or as part of, the traumatic scene represented in the dream (but not directly), and experiences of shame accompanied by dissociative states prominent in the day residue. I refer not just to the seriously impaired hospitalized patients who formed the main body of the formal study, but also to a number of less seriously disturbed patients in more acute traumatic situations seen only in outpatient practice.

Strikingly, when the sources of shame were identified and acknowledged and the shame was discussed, the patients began to assimilate the experience, and the dreamers became preoccupied with memories of shame-producing traumata in childhood, of shame coexisting with the trauma represented in their dreams, and—above all—of contemporaneous shame that often engendered immediate interpersonal conflict with intimates. Despite the considerable distress caused by the absorption in the trauma (which included significant narcissistic wounding), the experience provided great relief for the patients, who subsequently gained a stronger sense of continuity and an increased confidence that the shame could be faced and eventually mastered.

These psychotherapeutic considerations seem to confirm that the anxious state in the nightmares is not the bedrock of traumatic helplessness but is, rather, a situation further analyzable into childhood and dream-day narcissistic mortification that was screened by the restaging of the traumatic scene. The posttraumatic nightmares never generated shame but served instead as a defense against shame in the day residue. They reduced it, displaced it, or moved the dreamer into a scenario where shame was not generated.

The nightmares used the concrete circumstances of scenes associated with battlefield trauma or modified from those experiences to evoke one set of affects—that is, anxiety and fear of annihilation—while repressing awareness of shame-producing situations in the dream day. Wish fulfillment, then, was accomplished by the transformation of affect, not by hallucinatory discharge. By effecting this transformation, the manifest content of the posttraumatic nightmare is capable of screening a lifetime of traumata, the sequelae of which generate shame. I have dealt with the screening of early familial traumata in chapters 2, 3, and 4. In this chapter, I have emphasized that the manifest content of the dream and the affect it generates screen contemporaneous shame, rage, and dissociative experiences in the dream day.

The manifest content of the dream is part of a pathological structure that resembles a true psychoneurosis. That is, the manifest content is a dominant piece of ideation that deflects awareness from an even more disturbing type of affect belonging to the latent content. This psychoneurotic aspect (i.e., the manifest nightmare) is only part of the picture of the traumatic neurosis described here. The other aspect is the latent content, the actual deficits that show up powerfully surrounding the contemporaneous interpersonal failures of which the patient is ashamed. These deficits include self-absorption, neediness, rage, emotional numbness, dissociation, and intolerance of both closeness and separation—all of which generate shame if the patient is aware of them. The part of the psychoneurosis involving the manifest content of the nightmare and its attendant affect is an attempt to deal with that shame by transforming it.

CONCLUSION

The findings presented here do not, of course, constitute a complete theory of the origin of posttraumatic nightmares. They are drawn mainly from a sample of recently admitted hospitalized patients, but also they include data from a scattering of patients in intensive outpatient psychotherapy who had undergone trauma, usually attack or attempted rape. A truly comprehensive theory would require detailed phenomenological observation of many patients in widely different posttraumatic situations who have experienced anxiety in dreams, anxiety that they identify as being about the trauma in the dream. Nonetheless, in the sample considered here, the evidence that the posttraumatic nightmare was a screen dealing with narcissistic wounding—in childhood, contemporaneously with the traumatic scene, and in the dreamer's current circumstances—was both striking and ubiquitous.

CHAPTER 6

Delayed Onset of Posttraumatic Nightmares
Case Report and Implications

[with Carol R. Bley]

I

The phenomenon of delayed-onset posttraumatic nightmares is virtually unmentioned in the literature on trauma or in that on dreams. This neglect is due in part to the way in which posttraumatic nightmares are conceptualized, especially in the research literature on posttraumatic states. These nightmares are classified among ideation occurring in the wake of a traumatic event, so that the nightmare is considered to be as integral a part of the traumatic situation as is an inflammatory response to a physical injury. Posttraumatic nightmares are usually understood to be affectively laden stress response ideation, a "replay," as it were, of the traumatic event and as such more like an upsetting memory than a true dream. Since posttraumatic nightmares are usually felt to be more or less simple responses to trauma instigated by the impact of the trauma itself, questions regarding either the instigation or the onset of these nightmares are not only unanswered, they are for the most part unasked.

It is easy, therefore, to be held captive by language that assumes that posttraumatic nightmares are in some obvious way driven into existence or instigated as though from an external danger experienced previously and to lose curiosity about how it is that the past danger situation somehow exerts control over the contemporaneous emotional climate of the dreams.

Acute posttraumatic dreams and nightmares have, of course, been presumed from the earliest times to have both a meaning and a function that are obvious in view of the patient's overwhelmed and helpless state vis-à-vis the traumatic event. This meaning and function seem to be obvious attempts to deal with the external danger that the dreamer has recently faced.

We present a case illustration of a first occurrence of posttraumatic nightmares *12 years* after the occurrence represented in the dream. Issues raised by the clinical phenomenology of the case highlight and challenge some commonly held assumptions, often tacit ones, about the nature of posttraumatic states, posttraumatic nightmares, and the function of dreams generally.

Specific features of the case and of the phenomenology of the nightmare call into the question the notion that the sequelae of an entirely external danger drives into existence, controls, or instigates the nightmare.

We present details of the case to examine the special instance of delayed-onset posttraumatic nightmares as pointing to the activation of an unconscious conflict in the dream day or day residue. That conflict is itself a result of preexisting childhood conflict, and it generates and amplifies the shame and uncontrollable narcissistic rage that, in turn, instigate the dream.

II

The nightmare study arose because our attention was drawn to the high prevalence of nightmares in our population, especially in adult survivors of childhood abuse who suffered from nightmares. We have found posttraumatic nightmares, even the few acute ones in our sample, to serve a screening function for predisposing familial trauma, for an upsurge of shame that is contemporaneous with the trauma itself, and for narcissistic wounding resulting from current dysfunction in the life of the dreamer which served as an instigator of the dream. Despite the fact that most patients initially stated that their nightmares were exact replays of the traumatic events, comparison of the dream text with that patient's report of the actual trauma invariably showed dynamically significant differences even in the acute nightmares. These nightmares, then, were true dreams with latent content, dream work, and defensive function. Psychotherapeutic attention to the screening function of these nightmares proved a great significance in the overall treatment of our patients.

The psychoanalytic concept of screening derives from Freud's 1899 paper describing a memory, bland in content but unusually vivid. Freud subjected this memory (his own) to the same associative procedure that he used to analyze dreams. He found it analyzable into meaningful and disturbing latent content. The bland, vivid memory then replaced awareness of the more upsetting (latent) memory. Screening as a defensive function of memory came to be applied to all sorts of memories and *pari passu* with the evolution of psychoanalytic thinking, clinical material other than memories, for example, affects, actings out, symptoms, and dreams could be seen to have a screening function.

In our sample, posttraumatic nightmares, even those first thought by the dreamers to be exact replays of adult traumata, were found to contain details clearly departing from the patients' accounts of what actually happened and clearly deriving from preexisting childhood traumata or current-day narcissistic injury that found representation in the dreams.

Our sample, since it gave us a population of traumatized patients, most of whom were seen years after the trauma, gave us a good opportunity to observe phenomena that are not noted in populations defined as posttraumatic acute or chronic. That the trauma itself could not be seen as the current-day instigator of the nightmare was, in our sample, obvious. We will return later to the issue of whether or not the nightmare in the illustrative case was truly posttraumatic.

This chapter, then, is an exploration of the phenomenon of delayed onset of posttraumatic nightmares, found in about three percent of our sample of nightmare sufferers, and inquiry into the significance of this finding for our overall thinking about dreams.

We are especially mindful of the potential role of psychotherapy in the overall treatment of these patients and those suffering from posttraumatic nightmares in general. This psychotherapeutic work attains a depth that work based merely on abreaction, empathy, and superficial attempts at integration does not achieve. We have come to realize that in almost every case the conflict represented in a nightmare differs significantly from the conflict suffered by the patient in the dream day or a period of several days contemporaneous with the actual dream. The conflict in the dreams themselves invariably involved fear, which in the day residue generated shame and consequent narcissistic rage. Only as we began to appreciate the vicissitudes of shame dynamics and narcissistic rage in these patients' current lives and in the formation of their dreams did we develop an adequate grasp of conflict both conscious and unconscious in these patients' histories and in their current lives.

The present case was one of four cases of delayed-onset posttraumatic nightmares. (For another example, see chapter 3, case 1).

III

We present this case in some detail to highlight not only the significance of the nightmare but also the unfolding of a perspective in which the patient's life history and inner life appear in vastly expanded continuity. The clinical material is taken from a series of research interviews, not from psychotherapy sessions.

The patient, a 38-year-old, Hispanic male, was admitted after his estranged wife threatened to divorce him. He claimed that for 20 years he had been suppressing his hostile emotions. He had been using drugs, especially cocaine, for the last six years. He feared loss of control. Because of his outbursts of anger, he had been repeatedly imprisoned for violent attacks on people. A few months prior to admission, he was in an auto accident in which his leg had been injured. The contract on his job ended, and his wife of almost nine years separated from him. Immediately prior to admission, he had a fight with a man whom he almost killed.

He was a tall man, trim but very powerfully built. On the ward, his bearing was intimidating to the point of being frightening. When he approached staff physicians on the ward with demands, he would take offense if they did not drop everything and accommodate him immediately. His rage was explosive, and the threat of violence seemed very real to the staff. He appeared to go into an altered state of consciousness when he was threatening and abusive. At such times, he conveyed the impression that explosive violence was an imminent danger.

The Delayed-Onset Nightmare

He related a nightmare, repetitive over the last six years, which he described as recapitulating a scene that took place when he was in prison for armed robbery some 18 years previously. He was assigned a two-man cell with two bunks coming out of the wall, a toilet, a face bowl, a window only one foot square in the door, and shatterproof glass. Above the face bowl and toilet was an air vent through which one could hear people in other cells. Each steel bunk had a mattress, but no pillow, and Army blankets. He began:

> This guy, a huge guy, 6'6" or 6'7", with 22-inch arms and weighed over 300 pounds—he was huge—the guards put him into my cell at night. In the nightmare, we struggled. He threw me against the wall, and I came back again but to no avail. The sexual act was me masturbating him as he had me by the throat.

> He said he wouldn't rape me because I'd be the kind of guy who'd kill myself. But that's what he told me. It wasn't in the dream. There wasn't any talking in the dream.

He said that after the dream he had awakened in a cold sweat.

> I woke up stabbing this man repeatedly. Where I got a long machete, I don't know. I stab and chop into a thousand pieces. Every time he advances, I chop something.

He said, "In reality, I took a metal mop-wringer and hit him in the head. It was heavy. It weighed ten pounds. I wasn't going to let him spread the word about me and make me a target for anyone who wanted sex. I don't know if he's dead or not, but I hope so. It bothers me that I have no guilt. I don't feel any remorse at all."

In the dream, he had masturbated the man until the latter ejaculated; he struck the man with the machete. The actual event was somewhat different: "In reality, he went back to the bunk, back to sleep and waited till morning. He rushed out in haste I guess to tell his buddies. I didn't go to chow. I looked for a weapon. I waited when his back was turned. He was playing dominoes. I hit him. It was all set up by the prison guards. They know who's in what cells." It was the patient's conviction that the prison guards had deliberately set up the situation to humiliate him.

Associations to Childhood Trauma

His thoughts went immediately to a public humiliation by his mother when he was a teenager. Then his thoughts turned to his mother's open sexual escapades in front of the children. His father, a career military man, was almost always away from home, and the mother had intercourse with her numerous lovers in front of the patient and his siblings. The mother would beat him daily, usually in a humiliating fashion. As a youngster, he had tried to seek out his father. When he ran away and went to the base where his father was stationed, he found, to his horror, that the father had been running houses of prostitution. His mother told him only later that he was not this man's child but that of one of his mother's lovers. The mother had been involved repeatedly with different men at least from the time the patient was seven or eight. When he was 15, he impregnated a girl, the daughter of a minister. In retrospect, he said he had wanted to marry to get out of the house.

A Nightmare from Childhood

He remembered a nightmare from childhood. It concerned an event that happened when he was 12 or 13. The nightmare recurred till he left for military service at 17.

> In childhood, sixth grade, mother had a male friend who was homosexual. They played cards at our house. The homosexual, as a prank, would chase me two blocks every day. That was the nightmare. A jungle scene, bushes and trees [he had used the word jungle to describe the scene in the previous nightmare]. I ended up losing him. I had a fear of being caught and that motivated me to get away. Ultimately, I hid behind a tree with a two by four and hit him in the legs and beat him. He told my mother, and my mother defended me, saying I had a right to defend myself.

His immediate thoughts on the dream were confused. He wondered whether the man in the dream was his father. He had physically struggled to try and get away. He woke after the dream sweating, breathing hard, went back to sleep but was restless. He said he would awaken and then play possum as though he were asleep—"That's my paranoia, caught by a homosexual in a dream, being taken advantage of in prison in the nightmare." His thoughts went from being forced into homosexual encounters to working out in the gym and preparing not to be taken advantage of. Strength was very important. His thoughts then went to gangs and violence and his conviction that they were taking over the country.

When he was asked about worries of homosexual attack while failing asleep, he replied defiantly that he could deal with any sort of aggression.

Returning to the dream, hc said that he had ambushed his assailant with a two by four, hitting him in the legs and trying to break his legs so he could not run and telling him that he would kill him if he chased him. Asked whether his mother had actually defended him, he said, "Not really. She told the friend that he shouldn't be chasing me. I'd cry and ask for help, but then I was laughed at. She let me down. When I had a drug problem, I refused to go live with her and heal myself of drug addiction. I stayed here and submerged myself in doing stuff."

He was able to relate his rage and his high anxiety to specific fears about humiliation, homosexual or otherwise.

Later History

He was married for a few years before he volunteered for military service in Vietnam with the conscious wish to be killed. He was sent to Vietnam but was not given a combat assignment. He felt that he had been thrown out of the military unfairly and for racial reasons. Embittered, he had returned home to find the door locked and his wife saying that she could not get it open. He opened the door to find her with another man—another sexual humiliation.

He added that, recently, his second wife had become fed up with him, that he was a poor lover who could not satisfy her, and that if she had known about the homosexual episode in prison, she would have lost respect for him. The patient idealized his current (second) marriage and claimed to adore his wife and three children. He was horrified when his second wife left him. He lost his job. His anger brought him to the point of being out of control, he was losing his children. He felt that he had repeated his childhood experiences with his own children.

He noted that the delayed-onset nightmare concerning the sexual attack in prison had begun six years previously at a time when his second wife first threatened to leave him and when he had begun taking drugs very heavily. In retrospect, he said he used the drugs in an attempt to keep himself awake and thus avoid the nightmares. In his cocaine withdrawal, he would be able to sleep for a short time, free of nightmares.

He could predict when a nightmare was coming on. It was presaged by job tensions that occurred when he was participating in an all-male meeting and felt that he was not being listened to or was not being treated fairly or respectfully. We conjecture that these conflicts at work may have been similar to those on the ward that provoked his rage at imagined slights from male staff members.

IV

Discussion

We could find no mention in the literature of delay-onset posttraumatic nightmares after a period as long as 12 years. Freud (1918), in discussing the dreams of the so-called Wolf Man, refers to *nachtraglichkeit,* or delayed action, that is, the delay between the traumatizing exposure to the primal scene and the nightmare. The dream in question, however, was not a posttraumatic nightmare. Discussing traumatic nightmares, Freud (1920, 1933) implicitly assumes that in posttraumatic nightmares there is neither latent content nor dream work nor the tension-lowering function found of other dreams, which could be seen as a disguised representation of a fulfilled wish. To account for the function of these dreams, Freud (1920) postulated the ego's wish for mastery. In general, psychoanalytic and dynamic thinking about dreams stresses adaptation, mastery, and integration as the function of traumatic dreams generally. Weiss and Sampson (1986), discussing dreams of prisoners of war, notes that dreams dealing with actual trauma may occur after prisoners are freed, whereas to warning dreams precede capture and blissful dreams occur while POWs are held captive (pp. 122–127). Hartmann (1984) notes that posttraumatic dreams normally run a course of approximately six weeks before the repetitive quality blends with other dream elements. Chronic or intermittent posttraumatic nightmares are well known, though the basis for their chronicity remains unclear.

Some recent critics of Freud's views on traumatic dreams and dreams in general assert that Freud insisted that all anxiety in dreams was due to unconscious conflict (Fosshage, 1983) rather than to a confluence of contemporaneous disturbance and underlying conflicts that have been shaped by the patient's past experiences.

A good deal of useful work has detailed the role of dreams in problem solving (Blitz and Greenberg, 1984; Weiss and Sampson, 1986). Some authors have expanded notions of the nature of conflict from strictly oedipal conflicts (e.g., Jones, 1910) to include conflicts about aggression, helplessness, and fears of separation and merger (Mack, 1970) and loss of selfobjects (Blitz and Greenberg, 1984). Breger, Hunter, and Lane (1971) have studied the effects of the stress of surgery on dreams. Cartwright (1991), studying the dreams of recently divorced men and women in sleep laboratories, found that affectively rich dreams that incorporated the former spouse tended to "work," that is, to be associated with better coping a year later. Lavie and Kaminer (1991), in a study of Holocaust survivors, found that infrequent dream recall was better correlated with successful coping in this sample. Hartmann (1991), commenting on these two studies, conjectured that these authors may have used samples exemplifying different types of boundaries of the mind—Cartwright's sample successfully adapting with thin boundaries (affectively rich dreams incorporating the ex-spouse and frequently recalled) and Lavie's with thick boundaries (infrequent and less vivid dream recall).

Although repetitive posttraumatic nightmares usually do not successfully solve problems and certainly do not preserve sleep, they have been viewed as attempts at integration of traumatic experience with the patient's past—attempts that simply exceed the dreamer's adaptive capacity (Kramer, 1991).

There is a pronounced tendency in recent psychoanalytic and nonpsychoanalytic writings to ignore the problems both of predisposing trauma and of its disguise. Blitz and Greenberg (1984), for example, in their otherwise excellent review of narcissistic conflicts in posttraumatic dreams of veterans, concentrate almost exclusively on selfobject function and ignore the question of shame arising from the patient's conflicts that find their way into the dream.

We see our patient's delayed posttraumatic nightmare as a screen for narcissistic injury and shame resulting from predisposing trauma, from trauma contemporaneous with the events in the dream, and from narcissistic conflicts in the dream day that instigate the nightmare (Lidz, 1946). The dream, replaying an external danger, attempts to obviate the dreamer's shame at all these levels. In both of this patient's nightmares, a homosexual assault is followed by a violent and triumphant attack by the dreamer. The homosexual wish is represented as belonging to a man who sexually assaults the dreamer and whose attack is foiled by a show of force by the dreamer. We see these scenarios as obviating some of the shame resulting from homosexual conflicts and yearnings probably of a more passive nature, that resulted from the various traumatic experiences in this patient's life.

We return briefly to the question of whether a delayed-onset nightmare should be considered truly posttraumatic. The very question implies that the word trauma refers solely to the scenario represented in the dream, in this case the homosexual attack itself. We contend that the dream of homosexual attack and violent response is an attempt to repair narcissistic injury and minimize shame resulting from childhood trauma, homosexual conflicts contemporaneous to the dream scenario, and similar conflicts in the day residue. Since we emphasize the role of the dream work in handling shame from the latent content, we need not assume that this (or, perhaps, any) dream must necessarily be in the immediate wake of the event in the dream scenario to be posttraumatic: That is to say, we are emphasizing, using the present example as a case in point, the basic inaccuracy of the presumption that posttraumatic nightmares have no latent content and no dream work and are, at bedrock, "about" the scenario represented in the nightmare. Since we see the dream as attempting (however unsuccessfully) to solve a problem created by a lifetime of trauma and attendant shame attempts by externalizing the homosexual wish and following it by the dreamer's violent counterattack, we have no reason to disagree with the patient's view that the dream is posttraumatic.

The present case material strongly supports our contention that it is theoretically inaccurate to assume that the isolated external danger represented in the dream has simply generated an ongoing, dynamically static, physiologic, posttraumatic state that serves as an instigator for the nightmares. We must ask: What is the instigator of the nightmare? What drives it into existence? How can an external danger that occurred so many years earlier somehow exert control over the emergence of the nightmare so many years later? If it does, how does it do so? If not, what does drive the dream into being? These questions, of course, presume that posttraumatic nightmares have a function.

The tendency to link posttraumatic nightmares, even chronic or intermittent posttraumatic nightmares, to the enduring effects of a purely external conflict does not seem plausible in the case of delayed-onset posttraumatic nightmares that first occurred many years (in the present case, 12 years) after the external danger portrayed in the nightmare. It is not reasonable that the nightmares were instigated by a chronic or even intermittent posttraumatic state resulting from the dangerous situation if years have intervened between that external danger and the first nightmare. A delay of many years brings into question the notion that posttraumatic nightmares are connected in any simple way with either a chronic, unremitting or an intermittent posttraumatic state that is simply the result of an external danger.

It is also tenuous to make a simple comparison of the danger in the nightmare scenario with the current distress in the patient's life unless one presumes that something more complicated than an unmodified reaction to an external danger is taking place.

If we assume that a nightmare is an exact replay of a traumatic external danger and nothing else, then the dream seems to have no latent content and no dream work and to represent no wish fulfillment or defensive activity. Furthermore, if it is assumed that the conflict in the nightmare is an accurate representation of the dominant conflict in the patient's life, that is, as a threat of near-annihilation or a flooding of the stimulus barrier or a difficulty in reintegration after an experience of traumatic helplessness—then the appearance of the dream, the source of the anxiety, and the timing remain utterly enigmatic and appear to be driven by an external trauma that occurred many years ago.

If we assume, however, that both the external danger and the contemporaneous instigator of the delayed-onset posttraumatic nightmare shared a relationship to an unconscious conflict that arose from cumulative predisposing trauma, the data of the present case fall together in a more plausible way. The following is a sequence that seems to fit the facts in this case and in others.

1. Predisposing trauma reflective of an internal conflict has taken place in childhood; for example, In the case we have presented,

parental absence and neglect, beatings, exposure to chaotic sexual behavior, deliberate and sadistic humiliation, and homosexual attack in adulthood unprotected by the dreamer's mother.

2. That conflict, attempts to repair of damage, further rejections, and humiliations as a consequence of those attempts at repair, all condense into a characterologic resolution of the struggle, for example, the violent attack by the patient as an attempt to deal with his homosexual conflicts. In the present case, the mortification intensified when the patient ran away to seek out his father. This search, like other attempts to approach older men, was an attempt to repair damage or avoid retraumatization that ultimately gave rise to more humiliation and conflict, increasing the shame and intensifying the narcissistic rage. The unmanageable narcissistic rage created a gross derailment in the patient's integration and relations with nurturant others and destroyed the possibility of lasting corrective experiences and subliminatory channels. (The relation of narcissistic rage to guilt is discussed in chapter 11.) Consequently, a life style accrued that became organized around a characterologic struggle surrounding approaches to men and rejections by women, disappointment and shame, and consequent narcissistic rage.

3. A result of this central conflict is the increased likelihood of *exposure to danger,* in this patient's case, his being jailed and the likelihood of being raped. This is the external conflict in the nightmare. It becomes a facilitated pathway and screens other traumata because the actual event is basically an externalization of an internal conflict. Both the sexuality and the aggression in the nightmare scenario come from without as external dangers to be fended off.

4. The characterologic course continues after the initial trauma. In this case, the delayed-onset posttraumatic nightmare occurred when circumstances activated the same internal conflict that generated narcissistic rage. Destructive narcissistic rage, which derailed the patient's meaningful attachments and subliminatory channels, resulted in rejection, failures, guilt, and shame, which further amplified the rage. *The contemporaneous failure and activation of unconscious conflict and shame together with the upsurge in narcissistic rage are the instigators of the posttraumatic nightmare.* Furthermore, the nightmare serves a screening function by focusing on the external danger in the past and externalizing what is basically an internal conflict projecting narcissistic rage and homosexuality so that, in the nightmare, they come at the patient from without. The posttraumatic nightmare screened both contemporaneous and preexisting childhood traumata by a replay of the situation of external danger.

This formulation is plausible in the present case and in others in which the dreamer's chronic conflicts are typified by a clear-cut preexisting trauma that sets the patient on a characterologically determined course with attempts at repair, with further humiliations, and with narcissistic rage. This characterological response to conflict results in exposure to continued danger. This exposure to the trauma is represented as an external danger in the nightmare. This exposure is not fortuitous but, rather, is a consequence of the characterologic resolution of preexisting trauma and the ever-increasing and uncontrollable narcissistic rage that puts the patient into increasingly dangerous circumstances. Thus, the patient's character pathology has a large part in generating the dangerous circumstances that constitute the external trauma. The nightmares, in fact, shed light on the antecedents to this patient's intimidating and violent behavior if one infers that such behavior is in response to perceived sexual humiliation by men. The nightmares, then, are predictive of the patient's daytime aggressive enactments (Segal, 1981). The patient's circumstances are affected by characterologic responses to the homosexual anxieties, shame, and narcissistic rage and play a large part in generating the external danger that constitutes the trauma dealt with in the dream.

The only cases of delayed-onset posttraumatic nightmares in our sample concern trauma involving violence or combat. Exposure to both these dangers was the result of choice (i.e., volunteering for combat or seeking out fights) or of consequences of uncontrolled narcissistic rage that predated, for example, volunteering for combat or acting in such a way that imprisonment would ensue, as it did in the present case.

Our sample is, of course, too small to permit generalizations about the relevance of particular features of the clinical phenomenology. Furthermore, it is heavily biased, having been drawn from a population of deeply disturbed psychiatric inpatients and since the traumata in question involved violent situations into which these patients were propelled by some aspect of severe character pathology. It remains a matter for future empirical study to ascertain whether the same considerations would also apply to trauma in which exposure to danger is not a direct result of characterologic adaptation to narcissistic rage, for example, in car accidents, rapes, assaults, or witnessing or being the victim of violence. It is far from clear that delayed-onset posttraumatic nightmares occur in other circumstances. Detailed study of different types of trauma is required to explore the relationship of specific kinds of trauma to delayed-onset posttraumatic nightmares.

PART IV

ACTIVATION OF DISRUPTIVE STATES AND SHAME CONFLICTS

CHAPTER 7

The Sense of Inevitability Following Nightmares

[with Carol R. Bley]

In this chapter, we describe a type of nightmare, prevalent in an inpatient psychiatric population, that is experienced by the dreamer as signaling the inevitability of a catastrophe. This sense of inevitability leaves the awakened dreamer not only with the state of anxiety that is the hallmark of the nightmare experience, but also with the eerie conviction that the nightmare is, in some inexplicable sense, prophetic. A significant percentage of the nightmare sufferers in our sample (16%) reported that they experienced their nightmares as somehow prophetic. This phenomenon was sufficiently unexpected and prevalent to warrant inquiry and exploration.

We could find no mention of either the sense of inevitability following, or of conviction of the prophetic nature of, nightmares in the literature. The problem of prophetic dreams—that is, dreams felt by the dreamer to predict the future—is an age-old phenomenon commonplace in ancient writings on dreams and one acknowledged in the psychoanalytic literature from the start. Freud (1900) notes that such dreams tell us about the past and reveal wishes that, indeed, somewhat determine the future (p. 621). Zulliger (1934), in agreement with Freud, elaborates on the wish-fulfilling aspects of prophetic dreams generally, that is, as pointing "backward" to a wish not "forward" to a prediction of a future. He notes in his clinical material the elements of chance, of errors in memory, of workings of the repetition compulsion, of the breakthrough of unconscious tendencies, and of autosuggestion, and notes the gratification of the omnipotent wish to know the future in prophetic dreams.

A phenomenon closely related to that of prophetic dreams concerns the relationship of the dream to the dreamer's subsequent acting out, that is, of a dream that in retrospect seems either to the dreamer or to the therapist to presage subsequent symptomatic action that was detailed in the manifest dream. These dreams are not, however, accompanied by a sense on the dreamer's part either of inevitability or of eeriness. Roth (1958) notes that acting out manifest dream content occurs with consistent regularity when resistance to analysis of a dream is sufficiently high that it prevents a full interpretation of the dream. Segal (1981) discusses predictive dreams as indicative of disruption in more seriously disturbed patients great enough so that interpretation of the dreams could not sufficiently resolve the disruption which continued into waking life manifesting themselves as acting out.

In a more general way, Leveton (1961), in an insufficiently recognized paper, defines the "night residue" as the effective nightly reduction in repression and censorship that is not rerepressed on awakening. Such night residues may manifest themselves in dreams that are remembered, as well as in psychotic reactions, conversions, depressions, sleep phobias and rituals, and belief in the prophetic nature of dreams.

We came to appreciate the significance of nightmares experienced by the dreamers as prophetic only in the course of the study, so that data were available only on the last 63 of over 100 patients interviewed. Ten of these patients felt their dreams to be prophetic, although it was not possible in every case for the interviewers to comprehend exactly what the dreamers meant by prophetic or what specifically was prophetic about the dream. The nightmares were not prophetic in the sense of being precognitive dreams as parapsychological phenomena, although the patients, especially those with psychoses, tended to regard them that way. The dreams were closer to being prophetic in the intrapsychic sense reflecting an endopsychic awareness of an aspect of the psyche not fully acknowledged in waking consciousness. Accordingly, we emphasize the sense of inevitability following the nightmare rather than what the dreamer often insists is their prophetic nature.

It is striking that of the ten dreamers, eight certainly and two probably were grossly abused as children. Although there was some uncertainty about diagnosis and some patients had multiple diagnoses, about half the patients were schizophrenic, the rest being mixtures of characterologic and affective pathology. Substance abuse was common.

CLINICAL MATERIAL

The following clinical material illustrates the phenomenon of the sense of inevitability following nightmares from the point of view of unconscious wishes. These wishes have to do with vengefulness in the form of unconscious aggression; unconscious guilt as a reaction to such aggression; reversal of narcissistic injury; or withdrawal from drugs or alcohol. This classification is, of course, not exhaustive.

Unconscious Aggression

The most prevalent type of feeling of inevitability following a dream involved harm to a person close to the patient, who had no conscious awareness of hostility or, often, even had ambivalence toward that person. These patients invariably had been very severely abused as children and the aggression could be seen as a vengeful pursuit of justice for injury or abuse.

Case 1

A 30-year-old, single man with schizophrenia and characterologic difficulties was also a polysubstance abuser. All those difficulties complicated each other and had resulted in the past in his noncompliance with treatment and utter rejection by his family. The patient, one of eight children, had a history of physical abuse by both parents as a child. He reported four typical recurrent nightmares.

> *Nightmare 1.* [The most recent nightmare on admission.] I saw my brother in hell. He reached out for me. He told me to get my life together.

The patient commented: He was shot by drug dealers.

> *Nightmare 2.* My brother is shot. I predicted it. I dreamed it three times, and the fourth time on the day that he was shot.

The patient commented: He was killed by drug dealers.

> *Nightmare 3.* I see myself killing my family. I strangled my baby sister.

His associations: He recalled babysitting his baby sister. His mother had whipped him mercilessly because he left the child with a neighbor to go to work.

> *Nightmare 4.* We were in Long Beach. My sister lives there with my mother. My mother was in the kitchen. My sister was in the living room. I go to the kitchen and pick up a skillet. I had a verbal argument with my mother. My sister came in. After putting down the skillet, I grabbed her by the throat at the same time she is talking to me.

His thoughts went immediately to his family's rejection of him while he was in the hospital. They had refused to help him or even to visit him.

The nightmares reflect his rage at his sister and his brother and screen his rage at his mother for preferring the sister and rejecting him both in childhood and currently. He is also angry at himself, as is clear in nightmare 1, the dream in which the brother beckons him to hell. Although the dream obviously deals with his own death, his suicidal wishes are not conscious.

Commenting on all the nightmares, the patient said, "I have to be careful what I dream. I follow it out."

This patient had no conscious anger at his family members or at himself. Discussing his family of origin, which was rife with physical abuse and alcoholism by both parents, he noted that he did not think there was any injustice when he was growing up. The lack of conscious anger was replaced by the eerie feeling of the inevitability of the manifest dreams as prophetic.

Case 2

A 27-year-old, single woman was admitted with depression and suicidal feelings that had arisen after financial problems necessitated her moving in with her alcoholic father. In the course of her hospital stay, both her depression and her severe character pathology emerged, as did the history of sexual abuse by her brother and by other men. These clearly were related to her nightmares.

She had had nightmares since being sexually abused by the brother when she was eight years old. She was abused again at nine and had more nightmares. The nightmares stopped at 19, around the time that her mother died, and started again just recently when she was 27, when she moved in with the alcoholic and physically abusive father.

She had three repetitive nightmares:

Nightmare 1. [The brother who had molested her, in the dream, was killed in a car accident]. I'm standing there. My brother had a car accident. He died. I couldn't say anything or do anything. I kept calling him. I couldn't get to him. [She is asked to elaborate.] Only about three cars. They were going in the same direction. I didn't see how the accident occurred. He was lying there with blood all over him. Later I told him what happened to me [about being molested]. Someone was there and told me I shouldn't have. I couldn't see his face. He said, "Now they have got to be punished." I awoke crying and I thought it was all my fault.

This had been a repetitive dream since she was eight. It dealt not only with her molestation but also with her feelings of guilt; neither her anger nor her sexual excitement were conscious. She formerly believed that these dreams were truly prophetic but, in the course of psychotherapy in the hospital, got in touch with her anger, which had hitherto seemed as though it would overwhelm her. The eerie feeling of inevitability disappeared following discussion of the molestation. It was the first time that she had talked to anybody about it.

Nightmare 2. The guy [not her brother] that molested me. I see his face. I begged him not to let my mom die. She fell. I called for her.

Her associations: Her mother died right after that. Her mother was terminally ill at the time and the patient knew it.

The patient seemed not to be very much in touch with her sexual competitiveness with her mother nor, in general, with the destructiveness that she attached to her sexual excitement, her guilt about that, and the continuing confusion of sexual activities as somehow being responsible for her mother's death. Her brother and her mother died in the nightmares, but neither sexual wishes, aggressive wishes, nor conscious agency for the killing were present in the manifest nightmare.

Nightmare 3. [She said it was a replica of her molestation at the age of eight.]

Unconscious Guilt

One patient had dreams reflecting not only trauma from the past but also the workings of unconscious guilt. This patient was physically violent with the women in his life—and threatening to his female physicians—and was punished by unconscious guilt in his nightmares. They were indeed prophetic since these women inevitably left him. His aggression toward women could be seen as unconsciously linked to his vengefulness toward his mother.

Case 3

A 44-year-old man, suicidal and with sequelae of a motorcycle mishap that had required more than 20 operations on his leg, was transferred from another part of the hospital. He had nightmares that he said were always the same

> I don't recall the details except it's a feeling of having been left alone and deserted.

Asked if the dreams woke him up, he said that they did. They were repetitive and always left him with the same feeling.

There was overt violence in his history, the patient having many times abused women and gotten into fights. On one level, such violence seemed to be an attempt to control abandonment by intimidation, but it also was the reason that the women ultimately left him.

His recent admission had been prompted by his feelings about the death of an older man he had been close to in a domiciliary ward of the same hospital. The patient then made one of his many suicide attempts. He commented, "Everything turns to abandonment. I have the Midas touch [what he touched ceased being human]. I'm afraid to let people get close."

His first two marriages had collapsed because of his abusiveness. He had beaten his third (and current) wife, and they now had an agreement that he would live in some institutional setting and not at home with her. She still seemed ambivalent about the marriage. She would not let him live with her but had not reached a decision to leave.

Asked about his indicating on the questionnaire that he felt that the dream was prophetic, the patient replied, "I'm always afraid I'm going to be abandoned. Ever since I've been little, I've been left alone always." He realized that he was driving people away, especially people on whom he was intensely dependent.

At birth, the patient had been sent away to live with his maternal grandparents. His mother, however, kept his brother. He never met his father, an alcoholic. When the patient was two, his mother had another child, left his father at the time, and came with the new daughter to her parents' home. Again, she sent the patient away and kept the sister. An uncle whose wife could not have children wanted him and kept him with them from ages three to five, when the uncle died; the patient was returned to the maternal grandparents. He hated his mother and felt guilty when she died. She had been shaking with phenobarbital intoxication and was hospitalized at a state hospital. When he was 12, she made sexual advances toward him, and he had sexual relations with her until he was 15. He also hated his grandmother who was a tyrant, but he adored his grandfather. The connection was made between his closeness to his grandfather, his uncle, and the man in the domiciliary. His adoration of men was in contrast to his hatred of women—his mother, his sister, and his maternal grandmother, and their current-day representatives in the women to whom he was close and on whom he was dependent.

He was severely alcoholic and was violent when drunk. He had beaten up his third wife. His longest marriage, to a police officer, had lasted eight years.

His nightmares could be seen as posttraumatic because the patient had been grossly abandoned a number of times. But they could also be seen as predictive and emanating from his sense of guilt at the enormous dependency and rage he felt toward women. Underneath the almost constant rage, he felt guilty and unworthy of the care that he also yearned for. The relationship of the anger to the abandonment, therefore, was complex.

This man's style of intimidating through threats of violence and actual violence—narcissistic rage stemming from awareness of his own neediness, his shame, his personality incohesion, and guilt over his violent acts—suggests that the issue of abandonment was not only prominent in his history but also was something that he engineered in his current-day life and basically thought that he deserves.

Reversal of Narcissistic Injury

Another case demonstrates how a combination of wounded narcissism over a wife's infidelity was handled by wishful reversals in a patient also facing a sense of imminent psychotic collapse.

Case 4

A 35-year-old man was admitted after he had taken 15 tablets of an uncertain medication. He denied, however, that he was suicidal. He said only that he could not sleep. He was evidently psychotic and referred to his almost nightly nightmares as visions. He had many psychotic experiences.

He reported the following nightmare. The first, at times indistinguishable from his daytime experience, was clearly psychotic:

> I saw two people dead in a place that looks like a hospital. That made me think of this place because it seemed I was there in a crazy house. In the vision, there was a knife, and it looked life someone was hanging himself and I awoke thinking and feeling it happened there.

The second part of the nightmare dealt with his reversal of the helplessness he felt in the face of his wife's infidelity:

> I also saw my little girl screaming for her daddy, and a boy struck her in the back with something that looked like a pen or pencil. I tried to reach her but I couldn't touch her. I saw a school and a playground there.

His comment: "I must find her. She needs me."

He felt as though the dream were something that already happened.

His early history was replete with difficulties. He was the ninth of 11 children, and his mother had whipped him repeatedly. He left home at the age of 10 and fended for himself. He moved away from the city where he had been born and enlisted in the military service when he was 17.

He had recently discovered his wife's infidelity. He had chased after her. While he used the dream as an almost delusional rationale to chase after, that is, to protect his daughter, the indignity of discovering the wife's infidelity had prompted the need for the reversal of who was powerful (he) and who was vulnerable (his daughter), who was sexual, and what the nature of the danger from attack was.

His suicidal ideation had also been intensified when, recently, he read in the newspaper that two patients at another Veterans Administration hospital had killed themselves by hanging.

He experienced the whole nightmare as a vision that either could come true or that had already come true.

Noteworthy in this case were the psychosis, the history of abuse, the recent humiliation of his wife's infidelity, and his humiliation at being the one who was needy. All these were replaced by his preoccupation—of almost delusional intensity—with his daughter's safety. His conscious feeling was that of responsibility to his daughter to make sure that she would be all right. The nightmare, which was experienced as a vision and the basis for the delusional preoccupation with the daughter, allowed him to rework all these elements into a less humiliating view of reality that justified a quest to rescue his daughter.

He voiced fear that people around him, other patients on the ward, would try to hurt themselves. He believed in visions and extrasensory perception.

Withdrawal Nightmares in Chemically Dependent Patients

One of the patients—the only one who had no history of having suffered actual abuse as a child—had a nightmare reflecting his conflict over withdrawal from drugs.

Case 5

A 42-year-old man with schizophrenia was hospitalized for the purpose of helping him in his struggle against cocaine addiction. His nightmare:

> I was smoking cocaine and I couldn't stop. I didn't want to smoke coke.

His associations: I try to get away from coke. It comes after me. It is a conscious battle.

Concerning the sense of inevitability following the quality of the dream that he experienced as prophetic, he said, "Yes, I'll wind up dead if I smoke coke . . . I think the devil wants my soul." He had waking nightmares, too, that scared him. The dream experience was not separate from other psychotic experiences. His grandfather told him that his nightmares were a prophecy and referred to devils and demons. The patient said he lost his wife because of his drug usage. Although he was not directly abused physically or sexually as a child, he did witness his stepfather shooting his mother. He subsequently joined the military, wanting combat experience (a frequent finding in our nightmare subjects) but was not assigned to combat.

His is a withdrawal dream. There is a constant struggle experienced as a battle with "demons" over his drug abuse. The inevitable quality of the dream has to do with his wish to use cocaine, a wish he seemed utterly to repress and replace by the idea that the devil wanted his soul.

DISCUSSION

Our clinical material confirms much of what has been noted by other authors. The sense of inevitability, predictability, or prophecy, being based on repressed wishes unavailable to consciousness, points to an unconscious wish, and, if fulfilled, to the future (Freud, 1900; see also

Zulliger, 1934). That sense of inevitability, then, reflects a sense of internal awareness of a wish. The wishes in Cases 1 and 2 and the withdrawal nightmare in Case 5 illustrate this quite clearly. The imminent failure of repression and the emergence of sexual or aggressive chaos seems to be the greatest fear—that is, of sexual, sexually competitive, or aggressive acts either toward love objects (in Cases 1 and 2) or retaliation in the form of suicidality or abandonment (in Cases 1, 2, and 3).

What Zulliger (1934) calls omnipotence is actually omniscience, that is, in the dream that is identified by the dreamer as prophetic, that which initially is feared to be chaotic and unpredictable becomes, *pari passu* with the sense of prophecy, predictable. This omniscience, too, is, of course, a wish.

In "The Uncanny" Freud (1919) describes the sense of eeriness when repressed material is about to return. This eeriness or uncanniness also accompanies the sense of inevitability that followed the dreams. In several cases (not illustrated here) in which we could not grasp what the patients meant by the prophetic nature of their dreams from their content, it was the dreamers' sense of the uncanny, together with their sense of conviction that the dreams were somehow inevitable, that caused the patients to label them as prophetic dreams, whether or not we could see their prophetic aspect.

We agree with Leveton (1961) about the importance of what he calls the "night residue," the effect of lowering repression and censorship that is not rerepressed on awakening. The prescience of the danger of emerging repressed material terrifies the patient. The sense of inevitability derives in part from such material that has not been rerepressed and is felt by the patient to be in danger of being enacted; hence the sense of inevitability. We do not agree, however, with Leveton's assumption that the night residue consists of "repressed drives" in any sense that misleadingly implies that the repressed material is not connected with the day residue of the preceding day or the continuity of the patient's life generally. Indeed, the day residue and the night residue were intimately connected in our patients, especially in the psychotic cases. In Case 4, as with many psychotic patients' nightmares, there is little difference if any between the day residue, that is, the patient's conscious experiences in the dream day, and the patient's experience of the dream.

Our sample did result in hitherto unreported perspectives on the clinical material. One noteworthy finding was the high prevalence of psychosis in patients reporting a sense of inevitability following their nightmares (Cases 1, 4, and 5). This prevalence was not surprising for an impatient psychiatric population. Nonetheless, it did raise the question of whether the sense of inevitability that these psychotic patients clearly experienced as prophetic was not part of a more generalized sense of eeriness, referentialness, and confusion of boundaries that made it hard for them to distinguish dreams and nightmares from daydreams, delusions, and other psychotic phenomena.

Most striking in our sample, however, was the ubiquity of childhood physical and sexual abuse. Eight of the ten patients with prophetic nightmares reported having been grossly abused as children. For one other, abuse was uncertain, but likely; and although the remaining patient had no clear-cut history of abuse in his family, he had witnessed his stepfather shooting his mother.

It is possible that a history of abuse, with its attendant early environmental failure, humiliation, and deficiency of psychic structure, finds its way into the sense of inevitability that follows these nightmares in the form of wishes for structure, for vengeance, and for justice. That is, the strong sense that these frightening dreams prophesy something inevitable posits by implication a wished-for agency that provides structure and justice in the universe, that is, one that carries out such prophetic necessities. That wish is projected and is experienced in a disowned way as a sense of inevitability in a group of patients who suffer from the sequelae of severe environmental failure. The effects of that early environmental failure persist into adulthood and make psychic collapse and humiliation without offsetting interpersonal sustenance an imminent danger: in the form of emerging psychosis (Case 4), being lost in the world of substance abuse (Case 5), suicide (Cases 3 and 4) or the workings of unconscious guilt (Case 3). That is to say, the emergence of a vengeful or destructive tendency and the dreamer's prescience of the lack of internal or (historically) external structure to oppose it causes the fear part of the anxiety of uncontrolled internal chaos that awakens the patient, which that also instigates the wish for sustaining structure. *The wish is that there be a superordinate sense of order to the world that opposes the chaos, shame, and loss of control that terrifies the patient at the time of the dream.* This sense of inevitability, then, not only originates in the patient's awareness of his or her hostile wishes and characterologic tendencies toward vengeance, it also concretizes a restitutive fantasy as well. The wish for structure is a wish to restore or compensate for missing inner structure.

In closing, we would like to comment briefly on the obvious imperfections of the present study. As a sample of cases taken from an impatient psychiatric population, where most of the illness is chronic, the sample is certainly biased. It is neither prospective nor controlled. It is not controlled for diagnosis, for severity of illness, nor is it controlled for history of physical and sexual abuse, although it is clear that those experiencing the sense of inevitability of the contents of their nightmares had abuse far more prevalent in their history than those who did not.

Despite these inadequacies and the shortcomings in the data and design, we report a phenomenon notably prevalent in this sample in which patients somehow prepared for and yet disowned the sense of involvement in emerging internal disaster by positing an external structure, a sense of inevitability, and a feeling of eeriness relative to the emergence of their internal chaotic states.

CHAPTER 8

Observations on Nightmares of Hospitalized Rape Victims

I

Among the clinical advantages of attending to a patient's dreams is the illumination provided by the dream or nightmare of the dreamer's experience and inner world. This illumination is especially poignant when set in counterpoint to the dreamer's conscious waking experience. The dream not only reveals the deeper meanings of recent events and their overall significance for the dreamer's sense of psychic continuity, it also gives what may be clinically decisive clues to the expressive and protective (defensive) needs, both conscious and unconscious, with which the dreamer is struggling.

In the case of posttraumatic nightmares, the terrifying dream, far from being a simple replay of the traumatic event, both highlights the overall significance of the trauma in the dreamer's life and promotes an appreciation of nuances of the processes of breakdown and reintegration that result from the trauma.

These considerations have special relevance to an understanding of the experience of rape victims because those treating rape victims are at particular risk for assuming peremptorily that they understand either the full extent of the traumatic impact of rape or the nature of the traumatic and posttraumatic reactions to rape. Such assumptions are often not only premature but positively incorrect and place the helping person or persons at high risk to foreclose, dismiss, or avoid discussion of crucial facets of trauma and its sequelae on which the

113

processes of reintegration and recovery depend. Such premature closure, furthermore, takes place surrounding a type of trauma the extent and duration of which is often seriously underestimated because the rape victim is so filled with shame from the precipitous loss of personal and social integrity resulting from the trauma, and also from the awareness of posttraumatic vulnerabilities, that she or he does not speak out.

This chapter examines the nightmares of three psychiatrically hospitalized female patients who were recent rape victims. It is hoped that these case reports contribute to the understanding of the complexities and nuances of trauma in rape victims. The clinical material also sheds light both on the relation of dreams to traumatic events and posttraumatic states and on the nature of posttraumatic nightmares generally.

Both the psychoanalytic and the descriptive literatures seem to view posttraumatic dreams as direct replays of a traumatic event. That is to say, these dreams and nightmares are described as though they were stress response imagery more like affectively laden memories than dreams (van der Kolk et al., 1984). Posttraumatic nightmares, viewed in this light and considered psychoanalytically, are felt, therefore, to have no latent content, no dream work, or no obvious function, defensive or otherwise. Freud's (1920) contribution on the subject of posttraumatic dreams makes these assumptions (see chapter 5). He postulated the ego's wish for mastery of a traumatic situation that instigated repetitive dreams until anticipatory anxiety could be formed to somehow mend the rupture of the stimulus barrier that occurred when the patient was overwhelmed by trauma. Freud's 1920 work and his subsequent (Freud, 1933) revisions still assume—without reference to case material—that the dream scene is a simple replay of the traumatic event without latent content, dream work, and hence without wishes in the usual dynamic sense.

<h2 style="text-align:center">II</h2>

Previous chapters dealt mostly with a sample typical of our population, that is to say, mostly male, mostly combat veterans with chronic nightmares or delayed-onset of nightmares. The study took place decades after most of the original traumata occurred in this sample of patients.

Study of these nightmare sufferers demonstrated a clear-cut screening function of their posttraumatic nightmares (chapter 2). That is, in almost every case, the terrifying dreams themselves differed significantly from the dreamer's own account of the trauma, even though the dreamers initially said that the dream scenarios were the same as their memories of the actual traumatic event. My colleagues and I discovered in every case (approximately 120 nightmare sufferers, one-third of their nightmares being posttraumatic) that there *was* latent content, dream work, wish, and defensive activity.

Detailed study of these patients showed an unmistakable relation of the nightmare to childhood trauma, ubiquitous in this population, which predisposed the patients to vulnerability to adult trauma. Often this *predisposing trauma* had an influence on that patient's exposure to trauma; that is to say, the childhood trauma left a residue of instability and rage that were significant factors in propelling the patient to volunteer not only for military service but for actual combat or to expose himself or herself to trauma (chapter 6).

Posttraumatic nightmares were not entirely concerned with trauma. There were clear-cut conflicts in the dream day that centered on fragmentation and shame and differed markedly from the conflict in the dream scene. It was utterly misleading to see the nightmare as a replay of a traumatic situation that simply reactivated infantile helplessness. In the *dream scenario* there was danger (that is, fear), sometimes guilt, and rage or attack coming at the patient, but usually *a self-representation that was untarnished* (Eisnitz, 1987), however at risk for annihilation it might be. In the *dream day* there were *clear-cut and usually overwhelming conflicts involving shame and rage and an impaired and humiliated self-representation.* That is to say, the patient was disorganized, flooded with shame, and humiliated by his or her inability to be poised and to have normal generative adult relations.

We saw dream work and the function of the dream as involving a transformation of shame to fear, and a portrayal of the self-representation as endangered rather than humiliated. The dreams had latent content, dream work, and defensive function with wishes in the latent thoughts. Secondary revision was a notable feature of most of these dreams; the comment, "It was about Vietnam," was a last layer of defense whereby the patient assumed, often glibly, that the dream was indeed a replay of the traumatic situation that he or she had suffered.

The present material concerns nightmares of a small sample of women hospitalized shortly after they had been raped. The material extends our previous work to nightmares following trauma that is recent and that is not combat related. I have attempted in all three cases to capture in some detail the flavor of the interviews rather than simply to summarize the findings pertinent to the theoretical points being made. This method of presentation should help the reader to enter the world of these patients deeply enough to comprehend their experiences and struggles and to appreciate the pertinent clinical and theoretical issues in context.

III

Case 1

A 39-year-old woman was admitted for the second time since her rape a few months previously. On the previous hospitalization she had been placed in a sober-living home for recovering homosexuals but had been evicted from this placement when she was caught drinking on the premises.

Since the rape, she had had repetitive nightmares that she described as simply reliving her experiences of having been raped at 2:00 in the morning three months prior to the interview.

Her most recent nightmare had been two nights before the interview. She had had the same nightmare the night before:

> I was having trouble sleeping. In the dream, I was still awake and trying to go to sleep. I was lying on my side. A man or woman [was there].
>
> I couldn't move. I was trying to raise my head. I got my head up. Then, I couldn't move my arms. I realized there was nobody in the room. I woke up. This happened three or four times in the night on both nights. The worst was the powerful feeling of not being able to move. That was the scary part. The lights were off in the room. I remembered I had to lay on my back to go to sleep.
>
> So I had both my arms straight.

The interviewer commented, "You were dreaming about going to sleep." She agreed. The interviewer continued, "In the dream, there's nobody in the room even though you have a roommate."

She replied, "Yes, the girl in the room [also a recent trauma victim] woke up screaming and I thought it was my scream."

She elaborated the nightmare:

Nightmare 1. Tuesday and Wednesday when I dozed off, I'd feel terrified. A hard time even opening my eyes. Wednesday night, it happened three or four times. I put the light back on. I lay down. I took the sleeve of my robe and left it over my eyes. I left the light on in the room. At least I'd be able to see if anybody was there [this was all a dream].

This nightmare was indicative of her fear and vigilance in the alien surroundings. The interviewer commented, "You were dreaming about being on guard."

The patient replied, "Yes. Sharing the room with this gal. This refreshed all my experiences. Before that, I'd had no dreams for quite a while. In my nightmares—I'm powerless or I'm being held."

She reported another recent nightmare.

Nightmare 2. My father called me. Both cousins in Seattle had been killed in an accident. I remember crying in the dream. I hadn't seen my family in a while.

In this dream, the traumatic situation is displaced onto one in which she is not the victim and does not feel guilty, and she is united with her father. She said she had had other dreams about the rape, reliving the same situation but focusing on different things.

Nightmare 3. One night I had terror or fear. In it this guy is telling me he's going to kill me. No matter what I did, he was going to kill me.

She said this had actually happened.

Nightmare 4. I remember the pain. Internal pain and getting hit. The roughness of the man against my back. Reliving the pain again. And my back was sore the next day. I don't know why.

Her associations: "The flashbacks bother me more. They're shorter in duration. I'm wide awake. They scare me more. I feel out of control. The physical response is anxiety and breathlessness. I walk down the street. It could happen any time. I suffered seizures from alcohol, the same thing. I mean, you never know what might happen. I'm 100% vulnerable in the flashback for a few seconds."

In the recovery house she had had another dream:

Nightmare 5. I was sneaking around in the recovery house drinking about the house. I did that twice. [She had been evicted for that reason immediately prior to the rape and prior to the current admission.]

This is typical of so-called slip dreams, which are common predictors of relapse into substance abuse by persons in recovery.

The patient's description of the actual trauma was as follows. "Before it happened, I was depressed, I was afraid. I was drunk, but not to the point of not knowing what I was doing. It wasn't a blackout. I walked around downtown, cold and scared. I was depressed. I was trying to get to a detoxification place. I was kicked out of the recovery house for drinking. I wasn't aware there was anyone behind me. I didn't realize anyone was there. I was close to a separation between buildings. It wasn't an alley. It wasn't big enough to drive through. There was scuffling at first. I was trying to get away. All three of us. There were two guys. We were struggling. I fell down. I was struggling. They started to get control, one guy holding me. I started to get hit in the face, in the eyes. He told me to be quiet. I quit moving.'' At this point, she said that she wanted to discontinue the interview, but added that two men had forcible intercourse with her and then threatened to kill her. ''Before they started intercourse, they turned me over. Shoved my head down to the sidewalk. They were going for anal intercourse, but I was fighting too much, and they realized it wouldn't be easy. I got rolled back over.''

She had had nightmares as a child but infrequently. She was the third of four children. Her mother had married young, and had a son two years older than the patient, and then divorced. The mother then married the patient's father and gave birth to her older sister and then to her. Her father, an alcoholic, died of bone cancer at 27 when the patient was three. The mother remarried when the patient was five and had another son by that marriage. She is still married to that man. The mother was hospitalized three times for depression.

The patient never felt as if her parents knew she was there. One brother was a juvenile delinquent. Her sister was very pretty. Another brother, six years younger than she, was mildly retarded and dyslexic. Her parents were always busy with one or another sibling. She recalls hurting herself for attention. She hit herself in the eye with a book. She was closer to her sister than to others in the family, but she felt that, lifelong, she was not really close to anyone.

She finished high school and enlisted in the military because she did not want to be a waitress and there were few opportunities in the town where she lived. There was security in the military. Two years and a few months after enlisting, she was discharged from military service for being overtly homosexual. She had had her first homosexual relationship in boot camp. She was a staff person who became involved with a recruit. She has had intercourse with men but is not sexually aroused by them. She does not hate men, but they give her no pleasure at all. She has a severe drinking problem and dates the onset of her alcoholism from when she came out. Her parents are accepting of her homosexuality, and she has taken lovers home. She says she is close to her parents on a superficial level but repeated that she is really not close to anybody. There was no physical or sexual abuse at home.

Since the rape, she has startled easily, especially with somebody behind her or in an open doorway. She makes sure that her back is not to traffic. She has had interrupted sleep since the rape but not before, although she has always had difficulty falling asleep. After the rape, she had nightmares every night for about a month. She felt safe at the Lesbian recovery home to which she was sent after her last hospitalization. She applied for readmission to the hospital right after she was evicted for drinking.

Asked about her circumstances of readmission, she replied, "Saturday night I was drinking. I knew I had to leave the house. I was in a crisis state. I needed help. I understood that maybe I'd better come here. Even though I know my parents love me, I still feel like I was forgotten about. My pattern all my life. I want to be wanted and I don't feel worthy of it. Now every time I make myself vulnerable. I feel hurt. Loneliness is not as bad as being rejected. I've been living for a long time without love. Surviving, that is, not living."

She said that guilt is the thing she was dealing with most. "I can't let go of the idea that I was down there because of my own actions. I feel I was asking for it. There's guilt. I wonder if I wanted to get raped. My head is my worst enemy. What was I doing there anyway? I'm a failure. I'm almost 40 years old." She began to cry. "I feel like I have a lot to give. I wallow in the alcoholism." She has been different since the rape: "The walls are reinforced. I keep everyone out, not just men. I'm dying of loneliness. Every time someone tries to get in, I block them out. I reinforce myself so I won't have to be vulnerable. More since the rape. I've never been so aware of it. I always put other people first now, 'cause I don't think I'm worth it, not I cause I'm so good."

The interviewer, referring back to the nightmare, asked if it was really a struggle for her to let herself go to sleep. She said that it was. The interviewer continued, "You dreamed more of going to sleep than of being raped."

She said, "Yes, recently that was so." Asked about her dreams right after the rape, she answered, "Every night. It was a review in my head like a movie."

She recalled another nightmare right after the rape:

Nightmare 6. Cement against my back. My face rubbed in cement.

Her associations: The issue women deal with most is not anger but guilt. I feel like I'm less important now. I take care of others' needs before mine. I don't feel worthy.

Her guilt seemed to involve an awareness of the characterologic self-sabotage that is suggested by her history of repeated evictions and her exposure to danger. In subsequent discussions it became clear that this "guilt"— her imagining confrontations with what were basically self-reproaches—carried with it the notion that she was more in control of the traumatic circumstances than she, in fact, was. In this sense, her preoccupation with guilt served to defend against more deep-seated feelings of powerlessness and shame over both internal and external circumstances.

Nightmare 1 plainly deals with the dreamer's hypervigilance in the posttraumatic state in the frightening environment of a predominantly male ward. The nightmare can be seen as the marshaling of a vigilance that serves to prepare her for the possibility of retraumatization. Nightmares 3, 4, and 6, though they could be seen simply as a fragmentary reliving of the actual attack, may also be seen as fragments of preparatory dreams anticipatory of danger to a weakened psyche in an unsafe environment. Nightmare 2 displaced victimhood onto her cousins and, by explaining her isolation from family by something other than her own failures and shortcomings, dealt with her guilt. The slip dream, Nightmare 5, predicted the relapse that resulted in her being ejected from the recovery home and was, in all likelihood, instigated by the same feelings of shame, guilt, and unworthiness that underlay her lifelong self-defeating behaviors.

Case 2

A 36-year-old woman was interviewed seven days after she had been raped. She described the previous night's nightmare:

Nightmare 1. This guy, the police caught him. He's a vet and they brought him here. Looking for me. [This guy?] The man that raped me. [Who else was in the dream?] All the rest of the men that live here. [What were your feelings in the dream?] It felt like I was trapped and I couldn't get out. I can smell him. [In the dream?] Yeah. Even now. Smells like the sewer. His breath smells bad. I can smell his feet. He has body odor. [She looks to the ground.]

She had been raped late in the morning. She described what actually had happened as follows: "I was walking on the street. He was in the alley. He came at me with a knife. He held my shoulder. He made me get on my knees, put his penis in my mouth. When he was finished, he urinated on me." She did not know him. She added, "I'm dirty. I probably have AIDS. I feel used. I have this odor on me. . . . She continued: "There were lots of people on the street. He started walking with me. He asked me my name. He told me his. He told me he was there to protect me, and he wanted to walk with me. When we got to the alley, he excused himself. I thought that he was going to the bathroom or something, and he came out with a knife. He had said to trust him."

"He forced you to suck his penis at knife point? Did you think he was going to kill you?"

"I didn't think at all."

"That's understandable."

"No. I should have tried something. My mind went blank."

"Don't you think that's understandable under the circumstances?"

"No. I shouldn't have let it happen."

"What led up to your coming to the hospital?"

"He urinated on me. I stayed in the alley. He left. It was the next day."

"You stayed there all night?"

"Yes. This lady came in the alley. She lived nearby. She gave me cheese and beer and a blanket. She told me she'd wash my clothes. She came back. That's when she gave me the cheese and the beer. She told me she had to get to her brother. That really scared me. I thought it might be him. I ran. I called my therapist."

She had been in therapy for several months. The therapist had been helping her. She had not been hospitalized previously. She lived in a boarding house. She had a boyfriend who was addicted to drugs. She quit her job and went to a homeless shelter for women. She had had a job interview scheduled and a test for a job but missed that after the rape.

Her parents had retired two years previously and went to the Midwest, where her older brother practiced law. Her older sister went with the parents. The patient is the youngest of three in a close-knit family. She spent two years in college in a business curriculum, then quit under unclear circumstances to work at her own bookkeeping business. She was married for 14 years and had three children. The marriage ended at the same time her parents left. She did not tell her parents about the rape. Her grandmother had died three weeks before the incident, and her mother was taking the death hard. "I just said I had salmonella."

She described another dream:

Nightmare 2. In my room. He was on top of me. I dreamed that every night 'til last night. [Having intercourse?] No. He was on top of me, urinating on me. The knife is always there. Last night's dream he was here in the hospital, looking for me. All these other men here are waiting their turn. [That's scary.] Yes. A lot of men. I want the men to leave me alone. [The men are scary. I guess you feel very vulnerable right now and especially here on a mostly male ward.] I guess. You don't know. Strangers. He was a stranger. I can't [trust] anyone. Anyone could have a knife. I have to watch everybody. They come on. I concentrate on their moves. If there are too many of them, I can't. [In the dream, you know who to worry about.] All of them. At nighttime they are loud and boisterous. They seem violent. They're very loud. [You're very vulnerable compared with the way you were before.] Makes me mad . . . I used to be able to stare any man down. Tell him to go to hell. Now I can't look him in the face. [You are not like you were.]

No . . . then I get flashbacks out of the blue. I read my book to try and get rid of the thoughts, and I get flashbacks of his face for no apparent reason. I want it to stop. I have no control. I always have control over myself, and I don't have it anymore . . . I don't like being nervous. I'm never nervous. I can usually control a whole room full of people. Now I'm very uncomfortable if there is more than one person in the room. I keep looking to see where I can get a clear getaway. Very uncomfortable here. My therapist said to try and see if they can help me. I can't see how. All these men. I don't want to be forced to socialize with people I'm afraid of.

[Here you're not yourself. I guess you have lots of feeling about that?] The only thing I see, the first time we had one on one. I told my therapist I don't want to go to group. [Have you told your doctor that? I'm sure he's going to be sympathetic to your choice about groups or not groups.] My meds aren't working. This patient forces himself on me. The man touches my elbow. Then he keeps telling me to smile. Others do. . . .I'm sorry, I can't look at you. I'm not myself. It really makes me mad. I'm not being disrespectful. [You feel ashamed?] Yes. [Can you tell me?]

Embarrassed. I feel used. How low can you get being urinated on? People know it. Don't want them to know. I feel different than I did. I'm not sure I can look my daughter in the face. I gotta get on with my life. I'm afraid to start. I don't have any problems talking to the women patients here. I want people to leave me alone . . . I want to be left alone. [I think I can help see that that happens.] Thank you. Thank you very much.

Nightmares 1 and 2 are preparatory dreams that bring the rapist into the hospital (Nightmare 1) or the patient's room (Nightmare 2). They prepare the weakened and vulnerable woman, finding herself again in an alien and uncertain environment, for the possibility of another traumatization. The body odor in Nightmare 1 and the man urinating on her (Nightmare 2) speak to her sense of shame and defilement.

Case 3

A 41-year-old woman, a cocaine abuser and previously a patient on the unit with diagnoses of personality disorder with severe paranoid and depressive traits and a history of child abuse, came to the unit from another treatment program wanting to be transferred. She said that she had been raped the day before. The clinical interview took place when the patient was transferred a day later. She had had, on the two nights since the rape, the same dream:

Nightmare 1. I woke up seeing a knife at my throat. It was the same as the experience when I was raped. Helpless, scared, and freezing my ability of feeling my emotions.

She described the traumatic situation as follows:

"On Wednesday morning, these people I was staying with—I was taking care of the dog—I stayed with a friend. We weren't sexually involved. I slept on his couch. At 4:00 in the morning, somebody was knocking on his bedroom door. Two guys entered, one with a knife at his side, a large knife. They went to his room and up to his bed, saying, 'Where's your money?' Then they saw me. 'Oh, there's a white chick. Where's your money?' I didn't have any. The skinny guy came back in the back bedroom. 'Give me what I want or you're dead.' He was inside me having intercourse. The other one, with the knife, said, 'You suck me.' Then he said to the other one, 'You get off, it's my turn to get in.' They finished and said, 'I want you. You're going with us.' In the other room, my friend's roommates were on the bed with their hands around their necks. They were fixing to kill them and take off. I was scared. They said, 'Get dressed and come with us.' I thought about escaping. I was going to end up dead. 'Let me get a towel,' I said. I got out the back door of the house, and I ran like a bat out of hell. I didn't look back. I didn't know what to do. My keys were in my purse." [The patient begins to cry.]

"The black guy was chasing me. I ran into a door and broke my teeth. I said, 'Help me, help me.' This black guy grabbed me. I grabbed the flag pole. It's amazing how strong I was. I screamed bloody murder. People didn't open the door. The guy got scared and took off. I scared him to death. Scared the people in the house. Next door people were outside. They were scared, they were shaking. My mouth was as dry as it could be. I don't know them. I walked in these people's house. I called the cops. The cops came, said something about drugs and me being on drugs. I was so scared. People around said they saw a blue Chevy and told the police they just left. They went down the street west while the squad car came. They went in there. Some movement in the house. They took another girl hostage. The blacks threatened to kill these guys if they told so they took a girl hostage, Sally. They took her car. The cops said, 'You weren't raped.' Nobody believed me. They said, 'You smoked Thai Bud marijuana.' These friends lied because they were scared. Nobody believed me.''

The patient was frightened, almost manic, desperately seeking relief for her duress, which antedated the rape. She wanted to convince the examiner to help her with her difficulties. It had been agreed that transfer and a full-scale treatment endeavor would be undertaken. Her main preoccupation was not so much with the rape as it was with the fact that she was always criticized, that she was never believed. She felt that she had never been loved sufficiently. Her father never believed her. Recently, she had received a large disability check and used it all on cocaine much to her father's disgust. This typified many episodes of failure in her life and her feeling that her father never believed her, never accepted her, and never loved her.

She was one of six children, three of whom died in childhood. The other two were sisters only slightly older than she. She claimed that, growing up, she hadn't been close to anybody. Her mother could not get close to her, and her father hit her every night at the supper table in her mother's presence. Years later she felt rage at her mother for not protecting her from these assaults and for an emotional desertion that left her desperate for the approval of her father, and, later in life, of other abusive men. She felt close to nobody and saw herself as the one in the family regarded as the loser and the one to be picked on. At 18, she joined the military at her father's insistence, was married for 10 years, and then had involvements with abusive men. She suffered constantly from her difficulties, and conducted financial matters and relationships in such a way as seemed to invite blame on herself for her poor choices of men, her inability to work, and, most recently, her squandering her disability check on drugs. She was intent on convincing the examiner that what happened, that is, the dismissal by the police of the rape and attack, really did happen.

Although she said that the nightmare was about the rape, the nightmare scenario was not of the actual rape but of her awakening with a knife at her throat, certainly very traumatic, but also imaginable as an answer to the policeman who had said, "Nothing happened. You were just on drugs, you weren't really raped."

Not only had she not been believed or comforted, she was not taken to the psychiatric hospital or to a rape crisis center for an examination. This discrediting and being treated as worthless resonated powerfully with a lifelong pattern and with her characterologically entrenched patterns of relating to people in ways in which she was always the loser, the irresponsible one, the one doing something wrong, the guilty one, the ashamed one. After relating the nightmare scenario, she said, "I can't express my emotions or my feelings. Guilty. No one understands me. I'm always ashamed." During the interview, she was (understandably) preoccupied with her desperation and her need to get help, but also with her agitation at not being understood, not believed, and discredited by men—a lifelong experience exacerbated by her recent experience with the police and her fears that this would take place again in the treatment situation.

The dream work is evidenced by the selection of a portion of the traumatic incident for the scenario of the nightmare. In this scenario, she was endangered and terrified but not, in this brief span of time, humiliated. This "editing" in the dream work can be seen as a wish confirmed by her outpouring of associations and her pleas that she be believed and understood. The actual experiences of near-murder and forced intercourse are only the first part of the trauma. There were at least three aspects to the trauma: the rape itself, the threat of impending death at the hands of the two men, and the discrediting by the police. In her abreaction of the trauma, she barely mentioned the intercourse at all, mentioned very little of the fear of being killed, but dwelt persistently on the discrediting by the police who wouldn't believe her. This trauma resonated with earlier rejections and humiliations that always accompanied her childhood and adult trauma.

IV

A number of features of these dreams merit comment. I reemphasize that consideration of these dreams is from the perspective of investigatory interviews, not from the context of continuous psychotherapy in which more definitive work could be done on the meaning of the dream studied through associative material that would take place in the frequent sessions and a solid and sustaining therapeutic alliance.

1. In all three of these cases, it was clear that the dreams were not simply motored by the traumatic event in isolation from the dreamer's current circumstances. They were very much influenced by the encompassing and alien nature of the patient's environment. These women were hospitalized on a mostly male ward at a Veterans Administration hospital, and the anxiety about retraumatization, that is, attack or sexual approach or discrediting and rejection by men was very much conscious in the dream day and certainly amplified by the circumstances of hospitalization. Although this factor might be seen as a contaminant, limiting the general significance of the material, it also points to the fact that the dreams themselves, even though all three patients identified the dreams simply as "about the rape," reflected the contemporary anxieties of each patient's weakened psyche and her preparation for potential dangers. These dangers included sexual attacks from men and surrounded the patient's posttraumatic fragility, her fears of sleep (Case 1, Nightmare 1), her fears of encountering the rapist (Case 2, Nightmares 1 and 2) or men like him, or being rejected and discredited by others (Case 3, Nightmare 1).

2. The trauma was not confined to forced sexual contact per se. In each case, the rape was accompanied, as it almost always is, by the victim's very real and often sustained fears that she might be killed and that whether or not she was to be killed depended on the whim of the rapist. This *coexisting trauma* consists not only in danger, but in sustained helpless humiliation. The pervasive sense of vulnerability in a world now seen to be unsafe is a universal occurrence and one that usually endures for years after the rape took place.

3. Predisposing trauma is clear-cut in Cases 1 and 3. Although there is evidence of a good deal of premorbid psychopathology in Case 2, especially in the two years preceding the rape, there is insufficient evidence to conclude that there was clear-cut predisposing trauma. In case 3, the trauma posed by the discrediting and rejection by the police is at the forefront and stimulated spontaneous recollections of similar traumatic experiences throughout the patient's life. Predisposing trauma and its sequelae amplify and color the traumatic impact of later traumata (Moses, 1978; see also chapter 2).

4. The dangers of being raped and murdered were compounded by both internal and external factors that kept the victims from feeling comforted, protected, understood, and soothed. These patients faced legal procedures and later hospital care in circumstances that, even in well-intentioned settings, left them feeling unsafe, unaccepted, exposed, humiliated and thoroughly terrified. To this must be added the

self-reproaches and shame related to predisposing traumatic nurturance, which left each of these patients strikingly unempathic with herself.

5. The dreams concern not simply the traumatic and cotraumatic events but *the posttraumatic state* itself, that is to say, the hypervigilance, vulnerability to being easily startled, fear of sleep itself, and fear of the dreamer's own ability to judge what is safe and what is not and to protect herself from external dangers and shame and from judgments made about her by others. These shame producing vulnerabilities gave arise to overwhelming conflicts in the dream day that instigated the nightmares. These conflicts are, of course, amplified because the women were on a mostly male psychiatric ward. It is important to emphasize that these vulnerabilities in the context of a frightening holding environment greatly heightened an already overpowering sense of shame.

6. All the cases show ego activity that have to do with preparation for what might be future dangers, sexual and otherwise. For Case 1, Dreams 1, 3, 4, and 6; both dreams of Case 2; and the dream of Case 3 are preparatory dreams. Case 3 shows a dream that prepares the dreamer for blaming, humiliation, and dismissal. Weiss and Sampson (1986) have summarized reports of such dreams in prisoners of war. In contrast to dreams dreamed after capture, they were dreamed by soldiers in the sample he discusses, on the battlefield itself before the dreamer was captured. That is to say, they are *pretraumatic dreams*. With these women, the matter is more complex since the dreams themselves are posttraumatic and arise as a result of posttraumatic states in which the psyche faces a world now seen to be unsafe at every turn. But they are pretraumatic to the extent that they are *anticipatory of retraumatization* since they indicate the ego's attempt to maintain vigilance, the fear of the regression of sleep, and the preparedness toward the possibility of future attack (Cases 1 and 2), or evidence in "rebuttal" of the humiliating dismissal by the police—or by other men (Case 3).

7. There is in all of the dreams a clear relationship of the nightmares both to current interpersonal and intrapsychic dynamics. Case 1 concerns the patient's anxieties at being on a mostly male psychiatric ward, her lifelong feelings of unworthiness reactivated after she was thrown out of the recovery home recently, the posttraumatic state itself, and anxiety concerning a recently traumatized roommate. In Case 2, the day residue is plainly concerned with sexual approaches from men on the psychiatric ward and fear lest the rapist return to persecute her. The third patient's nightmare is concerned at least as

much with exculpation and pleading for the understanding and comfort of which she was once again deprived after a traumatic and humiliating experience.

8. Comparison of the dream scenarios with the patients' accounts of the traumata shows unquestionable evidence of latent content and dream work. For the first patient, the first nightmare concerns her anxiety over the regression of sleep. There is secondary revision in the second case; the patient said clearly that these dreams were simply different aspects of the rape itself whereas the actual dream text proved to be more complicated than this. The second patient reported anxiety lest the rapist be admitted to the hospital; she also portrayed a scene in which he was on top of her, urinating on her. In Case 3, the "traumatic repetition" is confined to the brief (albeit terrifying) segment of the traumatic experience that portrays the patient endangered but not humiliated. This selection of material is the dream work and constitutes, as it were, a rebuttal to her self reproaches, her reproaches from others, and her sense of shame. That the women themselves identified these complex nightmares as simply "about the rape" is evidence of a type of *secondary revision* that serves to simplify the dream and reduce its disturbing quality by relating it entirely to a past event.

9. Shame seems to be a major feature in all three patients. What the first patient simply calls "guilt" is a complex emotional situation. She asks, as though accusing herself, "What were you doing there?" implying that her motives might have had to do with the not formulated but clearly suspected unconscious wish for the trauma itself. This patient has a long history of self-harming, self-sabotaging behaviors starting in childhood and including her evictions from various living situations that made her feel secure. She hurt herself to get attention from her parents, was evicted from a recovery home immediately before the rape, and evicted from yet another recovery home the night before her current readmission. While the exposure to the risk of trauma may have been motivated by unconscious guilt (see chapter 11), the actual feelings of being unlovable, unworthy, and blameworthy because she placed herself at high risk for rape—and the fact that these feelings supplant feelings that might imply that she thought herself a worthwhile person—make the dominant emotion seem much more like shame than like guilt. The helplessness and powerlessness are likewise sources of shame, as was her intoxicated state at the time of the rape. She talks as though she were ashamed to realize that the behavior was indeed motivated by her unconscious guilt and her self-sabotaging behaviors.

The second patient's shame is obvious as she comments on the trauma and on her dreams and current preoccupations. It is not entirely clear how much the specific element of being urinated on contributed to the shame, since this was a deliberate humiliation accompanying the trauma of being raped at knife point. It was most unusual in our sample for humiliation to occur in the dream scenario itself.

The third patient's humiliation, not only by the sexual violation itself, but by the discrediting, blame, and rejection at the point at which she most needed and deserved solace and comfort added further shame that was both contemporaneous with the trauma and anticipated in future relationships in which she sought nurturance and understanding.

Another source of shame in these and in all persons in posttraumatic states resulting from human malevolence is the awareness that one's posttraumatic fragility makes one different from other people. The world is never seen as safe. One's own reactions, colored by fear and startle responses, are overreactive compared with those of others—and one's poise and integrity are always more at risk of disintegration in alien or unfamiliar surroundings. The common defense against this sort of shame is withdrawal, isolation, and constriction of activities. In the backdrop of these current shame conflicts that leave the patient feeling different from the way other people are, dreams replaying aspects of the trauma relocate the dreamer to the one situation in which her fragility, reactivity, and fear is truly intelligible. In that sense, the posttraumatic nightmare (Nightmares 1, 3, 4, and 6 in Case 1 and the nightmare in Case 3) can be seen as a screen that defends against the upsurge of current day shame by transforming it into fear in the nightmare scenario.

In all three of these patients, then, there is clear-cut evidence that theirs were true dreams, not simply affect-laden, intrusive memories that replayed the scene of the trauma. These conclusions—evident in the chronic nightmare sufferers who were combat veterans—were also found in these very acute patients.

These dreams were those of recently raped women with coexisting difficulties severe enough to warrant psychiatric hospitalization whose circumstances undoubtedly amplified their anxieties about attack from men. The material cannot be put forward, therefore, as at all typical of posttraumatic dreams of recent rape victims free of coexisting psychopathology and in psychologically safer and more supportive environments. The material is of great value, however, in pointing to *the posttraumatic state itself as a source of vulnerability, conflict, fear of retraumatization, and shame in the dream day*. It is clear from the dreams that the combination of posttraumatic psychological impairment, exposure to an unsafe and critical environment, and humiliating sense of helplessness—that is, an acute contemporaneous retraumatizing conflict—had a major role in instigating the recurrent nightmares. The dreams, then, were attempts to deal with the imminent sense of helplessness and shame in the face of which sleep itself often posed a danger.

The case material lends strong support to the contention that a treatment focus for posttraumatic disorders that is confined too narrowly to the traumatic event itself is too limited. Also to be considered are the meaning of the traumatic event in terms of the patient's life history and predisposition to traumatic disorganization and the effects—so poignantly illustrated in these two cases—of the shame and helplessness posed by the posttraumatic state itself. It is this shame and helplessness and the patient's attempts to control it under circumstances of increased emotional need that generate the almost continual conflicts and retraumatizations that are significant instigators of repetitive dreams and nightmares.

These three cases point unequivocally to the fact that the nightmares, of these patients at least, are true dreams with latent content, repressed wishes, and dream work.

CHAPTER 9

Nightmares and Substance Abuse

[with Carol R. Bley and Howard Fishbein]

I

Any connection between dreams and nightmares and the problem of substance abuse may seem to be of dubious value in an age in which attention to dreams tends to be associated with treatment situations emphasizing the exploration of intrapsychic conflict usually deploying intensive psychotherapy alone, and in which substance abuse is often felt to be a disorder *sui generis* and not one arising from or attempting to deal with intrapsychic conflict.

In drawing attention to the clinical significance of dreams and nightmares in the overall problem of substance abuse, we make several assumptions. First, we assume that dreams are of use in a much wider range of treatment contexts than is intensive psychotherapy practiced as a single modality and that attention to dreams does not presume a purely intrapsychic etiology of the patient's difficulties nor an entirely interpersonal therapy for treatment. Second, we assume that even though substance abuse, once it has arisen, must be recognized as a disorder in its own right and treated by methods specific to substance-abuse problems, it does not, so to speak, have a life of its own. The substance abuser never ceases to be part of powerful and often unconscious dynamic processes that strongly affect the course of the disorder and that are illumined by an understanding of the meaning and function of the patient's dreams and nightmares.

131

We see consideration of the timing, meaning, and function of dreams, and of the patient's attitude toward dreams and nightmares, as enlightening clinicians struggling to obtain as useful a view as possible of the natural history of the disorder at hand. Exploration of dreams in context provides an added dimension that enriches a clinician's appreciation of the nature of substance-abuse problems, the nature and timing of relapse, and the specific place in the patient's overall psychic life occupied by the inclination to abuse chemical substances and the struggle against this abuse.

We were struck by the paucity of literature on dreams and substance abuse. In recovery circles, "slip dreams" are known as dreams of persons abstaining from using substances or in recovery that indicate a struggle with abstinence and, perhaps, presage a relapse. Despite the prevalence of such slip dreams, we were unable to locate in the literature on dreams, on substance abuse, or on recovery anything other than cursory mention of such phenomena (Brown, 1985) or any substantive discussion of the relationship of dreams or nightmares to substance abuse.

Here we present, from our overall sample of approximately 150 nightmare sufferers, recent case material illustrating two findings prominent in the clinical phenomenology that bear on the problem of dreams and substance abuse: sleep phobias, and slip dreams and nightmares.

II

Sleep Phobias

A great many patients in our sample spontaneously told us of their efforts to avoid going to sleep for fear of having a nightmare (Leveton, 1981). Such patients either had nightmares virtually every time they drifted off to sleep or often could predict, on the basis of experiences of daytime turbulence, that a nightmare was inevitable. These patients varied in their reports of the relationship of their substance abuse to this fear of nightmares. A striking number of them abused drugs or alcohol to deal with their fear of nightmares. Some used drugs, cocaine especially, to keep awake and avoid nightmares; others used drugs or alcohol to create a posttoxic letdown state (crash) that gave them a few hours of nightmare-free (perhaps NREM) sleep in which they would be reasonably free of nightmares; still others simply drugged themselves into a dream-free state of sleep with drugs or alcohol. What they had in common was the overpowering anticipatory fear of having nightmares and the attempt somehow to control the emergence of their nightmares pharmacologically or by sleep deprivation.

We are, of course, putting forth this observation very mindful of the prevalence of the patients' rationalizations and alibis justifying their use of alcohol or drugs. We are not putting forward a theory of etiology of substance abuse, and we acknowledge that difficulties with substance abuse require specific treatment once they have arisen. We are not asserting that the patients' responses to sleep phobia are the entire basis for their substance abuse, nor are we claiming that, if the problem of nightmares were successfully dealt with, the problem of substance abuse would cease to exist. We point here to the clinical phenomenon characterized by a specific fear of sleep and particularly of sleep anticipated to devolve into frightening nightmares that was prominent in the clinical phenomenology and often spontaneously voiced by patients to whom we talked about dreams. Without assuming that the treatment of the nightmare disturbance would alleviate the substance-abuse problem, we have found that nuanced attention to nightmares, in a setting favorable to dealing clinically with those nightmares while simultaneously treating the patient's substance abuse, was helpful for this clinically prevalent finding. The patient, naturally, attempts to deal with the fear of his or her own unconscious conflicts as they emerge following the regression and relaxation of defenses during sleep.

Case 1

A 46-year-old man was referred to our program from a substance-abuse program because of increasing depression. He was a truck driver who had gotten yet another ticket for drunk driving, had lost his license for four years, and was thus unable to continue driving. The loss of his license disequilibrated his marriage. He felt uncomfortable unless he was a long distance from home, yet he needed to feel that he had a family. He voiced contempt for and utterly disowned his attachment to his wife of 24 years. He said he had married her because she was pregnant. There were three children, so, he said, he could not leave. The youngest daughter was 15. He thought he might leave the marriage in three years. He admitted that he could not get along with people and became very upset around them. He had not held a job for longer than 13 months since he got married. Prozac seemed to be somewhat effective for his depressed mood, but since he stopped drinking two months ago there was a dramatic upsurge in his nightmares.

Over the 15 years beginning with his Vietnam experiences and ending eight years previously, about once every six months, he would, with the premonition that he was likely to have a nightmare, stay awake, sometimes for several days, and simply go to work without sleeping for fear of lapsing into a nightmare. He feared having one of the same recurrent nightmares.

For the last eight years he had been drinking to avoid nightmares and to drug himself to sleep. He had dealt with his nightmares in part by drinking. When he was drunk, he had few nightmares. When he stopped drinking, the nightmares increased. The nightmares were all manifestly concerned with combat experiences that he said had actually happened.

Nightmare 1. He saw a Republic of Vietnam soldier nailing a 12-year-old boy to a tree because they thought he was a Viet Cong. The patient felt helpless and woke up feeling that he was cowardly and should have saved the boy. He was depressed.

Nightmare 2. Mortar fire, the troops being overrun. Bee hives, huge barreled canons filled with pointed buckshot, were being aimed at the Viet Cong.

Nightmare 3. He was holding a dead friend in his arms. This man had just received news that his wife had a child. They had been on guard duty together. This man had said, "There's something wrong here." Next morning everything was quiet. Then the unit was overrun. He had said, "Put your helmets on." The patient discovered him with a huge hole in the side of his head, dead.

Asked about his life history, the patient said that he had been told that he was adopted out at birth and lived with an uncle and a grandmother. His mother had tuberculosis. He had met his father only twice. He went back to live with his mother and his stepfather when he was five. He was the third child of his natural parents, but there were two younger step-siblings who, he felt, were much better treated. He recalled no physical or sexual abuse or alcoholism. He was emotionally distanced from them. He said that they had done the best they could raising the family. He had left high school only a few months before graduation at the age of 18 and joined the military; he had gotten into so much trouble for fighting and for drinking that he was about to be expelled, and so he left and volunteered for Vietnam.

By his own admission, the combat situation in Vietnam suited him perfectly. He could not identify what or at whom he had been so angry before he enlisted, but, in combat, he felt whole for the first and only time in his life. (For illustration and discussion of similar cases, see chapter 2).

He seemed to have very little access to the workings of his inner life. The interviewer attempted to link the crucifixion dream (Nightmare 1) with (1) his rage at his younger half-siblings, who had received preferential treatment from the parents and at whom he might be angry; (2) his rage at his own children, especially his son with whom he fought constantly; and, most important, (3) his feelings about himself, as the one sacrificed by his family. The patient could make no further connections in his own life history to sacrificed children or to those who sacrificed them, but then said he was upset by the session and that the interviewer was prying.

Nightmare 1 portrays a scene that seems to resonate with, and to screen, all his feelings about children (perhaps siblings, his own children, or himself) being unjustly persecuted and treated as though they were enemy forces and, finally, sacrificed. Nightmare 2 rationalizes a dangerous world and his own preparedness to attack. The third nightmare, portraying a father separated from his new family and killed, may correspond to the dreamer's rageful feelings about his father, his stepfather, or himself as a father and husband seen in the context of a family life until recently always kept at a distance but never given up. The patient's nightmares—and his fear of having them—pointed to the underlying but unacknowledged murderous rage that had propelled him out of his family environment, first into military combat and later into his occupation as a truck driver, which allowed him to distance the family and people generally, getting far enough away to keep his rage and his depression in abeyance.

Case 2

A 51-year-old man presented for admission two weeks after a suicide attempt with drugs. He was a nurse anesthetist who had not worked since sustaining a back injury 10 years earlier that had required multiple surgeries. He had nightmares and said that he drank so that he would not have them. They were particularly frequent when he withdrew from alcohol. He drank and avoided sleep so that he would not have nightmares. He had had trouble with alcohol for 38 years, since he was 13, and with drugs, cocaine and heroin especially, for 10 years.

Initially, he claimed to have become suicidal because of his drinking problem, his failures in life, and his nightmares. One nightmare is as follows:

Nightmare 1. I dream about sexual abuse by my cousin who was 15 years at the time and by my father as well. My dad was alcoholic. I was age 12 or 13. He came in and sexually abused me.

The patient was vague about what had actually transpired, and he was asked to discuss the scenario in the nightmare:

Nightmare 2. He comes in and I'm sleeping and he fondles my genital area and he wakes me up.

The examiner, asking about the dreamer's sexual arousal, was told:

Yes. I tried to discourage him. He said, "This is okay" and if I tell my mother, he is going to deny it and there is going to be a lot of problems in the family.

This was a nightmare that had recurred off and on since two weeks after the incident happened. The abuse continued for about two to three years. The nightmares woke him up screaming, crying, feeling ashamed, fearful, and used.

The patient reported continued abuse, physical and sexual, by his father. The father also drank and beat up the mother. The patient had a sister, six years younger, from whom he was now alienated. He tended to idealize his mother and his relationship with her and said he often tried to stick up for her and keep the father from beating her. His sister, he said, was the apple of father's eye. The father would do anything to please her.

Recounting the story of his life, the patient described a miserable adolescence. He finished high school and entered the military to get away from his father. He was in the service eight years, did good work, but drank heavily. He had apparently favorably impressed his superiors so they did not take punitive action for his drinking but gave him a general discharge with advice not to reenlist. After his discharge, he worked as a cook, put himself through nursing school, and became a nurse anesthetist.

Questioned further, he showed distinct signs of posttraumatic stress—he was easily startled, he felt alien in his surroundings, upset, and preoccupied and relived the experiences of the childhood and, perhaps, subsequent traumata.

The patient had had a marriage that lasted for five years, ending 22 years prior to his admission. It ended abruptly when he got drunk and beat his wife, whom he described as an understanding psychiatric nurse. He was hospitalized. The wife filed for divorce, and he has never seen her or his son since then. He is also alienated from his sister. He apparently had had many arguments with the sister and was horrified when she compared him to his father. The sister also had a drinking problem.

When the examiner tactfully asked about the patient's having an erection in the dream and his struggles with homosexuality, the patient opened up a floodgate of information that he said he had never revealed in 38 years. He said he struggled constantly with homosexual desires. After the sexual abuse by his father, he was indeed sexually excited. During this same period of time, he had several incidents of mutual masturbation with a neighbor boy to whom he had been attracted. His thoughts then went to his cousin, an overt homosexual two years older than he. That cousin had forced sexual relations, usually mutual masturbation on the patient, again under threats that there would be reprisals if the patient told anybody.

The patient had struggled in high school with homosexual desires, which he did not acknowledge at first. He said that he had been so ashamed of himself after the abuse that he did not want to take a shower, did not take gym in school, and got into trouble with the authorities. He later admitted to wrestling with homosexual desires, as he subsequently did when his marriage broke up.

After the marriage ended, he led an isolated, alcoholic existence, not getting very close to anybody. After his father's death from cancer, he made a serious suicide attempt while driving. He later told the interviewer that it was as a result of this driving mishap, not through a fall in the operating room (as he had claimed), that his back had become disabled.

He told himself that he drank and avoided sleep because of "nightmares" but had very little conscious awareness that he wrestled almost constantly with his homosexual impulses. He came into the interview wearing a prominent crucifix and talked about his Catholic upbringing and his repugnance for his homosexual struggles. The nightmare, recurring as it had for the 38 years since he was first abused sexually, screened his ongoing struggles with homosexual desires by representing them as passive reactions to past coercion by overpowering abusers. In that way, his current struggles could be disowned and his perturbation attributed to past abuse rather than present desire and conflict.

Case 3

A 46-year-old divorced man was readmitted after a long bout of drinking. He had had nightmares about twice weekly during the period he had been sober and, in part to deal with the nightmares, had begun drinking heavily when his divorce became final in 1979. He had repetitive nightmares. Typical of this was:

> *Nightmare 1.* I was condemned to be hanged, although it was unclear why. [He is asked to elaborate.] I walk up the steps to the gallows. There are no people that I recognize.

When he was asked about hanging, his thoughts went to his grandfather, who had hanged himself.A giant of a man, 6'7", his grandfather was 60, blind and had inoperable cancer. The patient's parents never acknowledged the reason for the grandfather's death, and the patient did not learn until he was 17 that his grandfather had committed suicide.

The patient felt himself to be a disappointment to his father. Both his father and his grandfather were graduates of the same prestigious college. The patient had been a C+ student at a less renowned college but dropped out after a year and went into military service. It is unclear why he had left school. He said that he had felt a good deal of rage at his lack of nurturance at home.

Shortly after his enlistment, when he was home on leave, he drove into a tree deliberately while going 75 miles per hour. He did not know why he was suicidal and was ashamed of himself. He felt he was a disappointment to his father. Detailed interviewing failed to make clear his reasons for wanting to commit suicide. He had made a number of suicide attempts, all by trying to hang himself, and had recurrent thoughts of hanging himself.

Asked further about the nightmare, he said that the hanging might be a way of punishing people by showing them how much he had suffered and might be an identification with his grandfather. It might relate to the aspirations of his father and grandfather, both of whom had enjoyed success in college.

The nightmares occurred about twice weekly, usually between 4:00 and 5:00 a.m. He had no childhood sleep disorder but did have some nightmares as a child. He could not predict when he might have a nightmare.

He would try to avoid sleep: "I lie down. I have difficulty closing my eyes. I don't get tired. I sleep two hours. I try to wake myself up. This has gone on for two weeks or so. I drink alcohol just to pass out. I don't have nightmares. When I'm drinking, I sleep 12 to 13 hours a day."

The patient was the eldest of three children; he had two younger sisters. He was somewhat close to his youngest sister but not to either parent or the oldest sister. Although his father and his mother did hit him, there was no alcoholism and no sexual abuse. He reported his parents' distant, unnurturant attitude toward him, as though he were an employee. He wondered if perhaps this was why he had such trouble as an employee. He had high aspirations and even sold prestigious cars in San Francisco; but, even though he was successful, he drank heavily and constantly felt like a failure.

He had had one marriage, which lasted for six or seven years. His wife, herself a heavy drinker, moved out of their home and into her parents' home. His discussion of why the marriage had ended was, like his discussion of his suicidality, shallow and explained nothing. He did feel that he deserved to be punished but he was not sure why.

He did not connect joining the military during the Vietnam War with a wish to die, although he made a suicide attempt shortly thereafter. He had few personal friends and poor relationships with women, and went downhill when a five-year relationship ended five years previously, at which time he was first admitted to a psychiatric hospital.

This man seemed at the time to be depressed and to have a chemical dependency problem and a personality disorder. He had difficulty relating to superiors but did not talk very much about that problem, nor did he talk about his sense of shame. He did say that his life was going nowhere. Though he related his nightmares to suicidal wishes, he had never attempted or committed suicide in the nightmare scenarios. That in his nightmare he was *always about to be hanged,* and usually *in the presence of strangers,* may be an attempt to deal with his sense of shame.

It was only on a subsequent admission over a year later that the patient admitted to the longstanding psychotic symptoms that, for many years, had made him see himself as having a hopeless and deteriorating illness—like his grandfather's cancer—and identify with the sense of failure, disgrace, and hopelessness that had driven his grandfather to suicide by hanging.

All of these nightmares represent, but also screen, deep, partially unconscious struggles with which the dreamer struggled powerfully and daily, but of which the dreamer was only partly aware. The first patient's struggles with rageful and conflicted dependency, so evident from his childhood history and his contempt, ragefulness, and distancing from his family of procreation, are highlighted strongly by dreams that he experienced consciously simply as "about Vietnam." The second patient's constant struggle with homosexual desires was transformed into a replay of passive homosexual abuse decades earlier. The third patient's hidden and undisclosed psychosis was seen by himself unconsciously as confirming an identification with the grandfather who committed suicide by hanging. In each case, the "sleep phobia" was in response to overwhelming conflict consciously and daily experienced at one level, but warded off from the dreamer's full awareness by the transformations accomplished by the dream work that, in each case, made the dream seem like something remote and disconnected from the patient's almost constant struggles for self-respect. (For another example, see chapter 6.)

Slip Dreams and Nightmares

Slip dreams are commonly recognized in recovery circles. We found mention of such phenomena (Brown, 1985) but no detailed discussion of them. On the obvious level of manifest content, slip dreams are a sign indicating a wish to resume substance abuse, the temptation to use the substance, and the patient's risk for relapse into substance abuse. Taken as a simple sign flagging the risk of relapse, they may be of some use clinically. We wish to draw attention, however, to the usefulness of studying such dreams in more detail and to look carefully at the nuances of the manifest content and, then, to go beneath the surface to the latent content; that is to say, to treat these dreams as mental products to be analyzed dynamically.

In the manifest content, the details very much give a clue to the specifics of the patient's struggle, which goes beyond the simple issue of temptation or wish to use substances. In addition to these manifest details, we assume there is latent content to the dreams that provides useful insights into their overall clinical significance; that is to say, dreams are true symptoms and compromise formations, not just signs. We look to the dream as an instance of a much more general phenomenon of self-sabotage, relapse, the unconscious wish to fail or be punished, and changes in the nature of attachments to supportive persons that the patient uses not only in dreams but in waking life. These dreams represent, then, not only an upsurge in the struggle against the temptation to abuse substances but also conflict of one sort or another that, in the dream, is represented as "solved," as it were, by drinking or drug abuse, but that itself engenders (as does substance abuse itself) other and perhaps more serious conflicts.

Our sample is, of course, at the more severe end of the spectrum of psychopathology. This sample is confined to psychiatric inpatients, hospitalized not only for severe psychopathology other than substance abuse, but for substance abuse itself that had gotten out of control; that is to say, a population heavily skewed toward patients who had already slipped. Furthermore, since the main thrust of our study was nightmares, not simply dreams, we have a doubly biased sample, but nonetheless a clinically striking one, of the phenomenon of slip dreams. An overall and balanced study of such dreams might better take place outside a hospital setting, with a less sick population, and using dreams as well as nightmares as objects of study.

Case 4

A 35-year-old man, separated from his third wife, described a relapse that had taken place two days before Mother's Day, some three weeks prior to the interview. He had had serious problems with substance abuse for most of his adult life and had failed in many attempts at recovery over the last six years. He had a nightmare on the night prior to his interview.

> *Nightmare 1.* Last night I dreamed that I was with persons who I know and some were unknowns. The dream involved the use of drugs. It was an attempt by me to get high, and the high never materialized. I was with some people—my brother-in-law who used to deal drugs and marijuana. I was using cocaine in a pipe, inhaling and smoking. I never got high. There was lots of residue in the pipe.

He described a dream that he had had two days prior to getting high while on a pass from the hospital three weeks previously:

> *Nightmare 2.* It was two days before I last got high, Wednesday, May the 5th. I used Friday, May the 7th. The day after the dream, I had an appointment with the Salvation Army. My drug problem tried to kick in. I'm in a fog. It lingers and lingers. It gets stronger. This was the morning after the dream. I had been sober 30 days. The emotions of the dream carried over. I woke up with an erection. The dream was like a nightmare. I woke up thanking God it's not a reality. I don't remember the full dream. There was sex in the dream. I have emissions in the dream, especially such a long time without sex. The clothes are messed up. There is nothing I can do. No particular woman. Getting ready to—well, I just smoked some cocaine. It's a pattern I have. I manipulate drugs for sex. This never involves my wife but always other women. I pick up urges to get high that come from my subconscious. I don't have any conscious yearning. That Wednesday, I saw this woman from the dream. Damn it, I'm going to get high, I said. I wouldn't let myself admit it. I tried to fight it. That's the way I am. I deny that part of me wants to get high. The day before the dream, I didn't think straight. My mind and body were pulling at me. I fought it off. The day I had the

dream, I noticed the urges. I was thinking about it more and more. I felt it taking over. I went back to the ward. That was the day I had the dream. The day after the dream, Thursday, I was afraid to go downtown. I didn't want to. didn't want to take chances. It was really a struggle. I came back to the ward on Thursday. I didn't go downtown to get Mother's Day gifts. On Friday, everything was perfect. I had the screening at the long-term drug program. It was stressful. I started getting anxious. They made us wait almost an hour. It was a long time. I wasn't angry at them. Later, I got a ticket on the Metro Rail for smoking. I called. My wife wasn't there. I didn't know what she was up to. I wasn't sure. I left the interview for the drug program, took the bus to downtown, took the Metro Rail, went home. She wasn't there. I was frustrated. I called. Nobody answered. I stopped fighting. It came on. My body chemistry changed. This time, there was little resistance.

Asked about the interview at the long-term rehabilitation program, the patient responded, "They turned me down. About the feelings, I don't know."

He continued, "Sex had a big part to play in it. My insecurities with my wife. If she doesn't get her orgasm, I feel guilty. My first wife was unfaithful. Sex wasn't good. We don't trust each other. Sex. Not to go through the pressure with my wife. Not the personal relationship. I used on Friday. Got off the Metro Rail, went home. My wife wasn't there. I went to my mom's house. Used drugs on Friday. I think my subconscious overrode my conscious mind."

He talked about other nightmares.

Nightmare 2. Lots of other dreams. People chasing me. It's always a struggle.

The patient had been attempting recovery for the past six years and was quite psychologically minded. He said he had had the nightmare on the night that he did "because of unresolved situations in my life." He repeated that view several times on the nightmare questionnaire that was preparatory to the interview. Asked why he thought he had nightmares, he wrote, "My subconscious is living the experiences while I sleep."

He blamed himself for his many problems with substance abuse. He had had two previous marriages and was separated from his present wife and argued incessantly with her sons by a previous marriage. His brother-in-law, a drug dealer, repeatedly drew him into substance abuse. He had numerous job failures, was a disappointment to his family, and had difficulties dating back to college, where he was dropped from an athletic scholarship for drug use for what he called a nervous breakdown.

He was one of four children born to a mother who was not married to his father. His stepfather beat him, his mother, and his sister. There was no drug abuse in the family. He turned to alcohol in high school. He suffered what he called a nervous breakdown in college. He failed classes, lost his scholarship, and turned to increasing abuse of cocaine, heroin, methadone, and alcohol. He had many "slip" dreams in the years when he was trying to overcome drugs. In the current one, the struggle is represented by his using cocaine but somehow not getting high.

Case 5

A 35-year old, single man who, since the age of four, had had intense dreams and nightmares that intensified at the age of 28, when his cocaine habit started, was admitted for depression and cocaine use. He was depressed over the deteriorating course of his life, which he felt was out of control because of his use of cocaine.

The last nightmare took place the night before the interview and was typical of his almost nightly repetitive nightmares:

Nightmare 1. They just about all the time have a woman in them who will trade sex for drugs. I really don't have these dreams until I try to get my life together. They are accompanied by upset stomach and headaches, and I guess the need or want of drugs. I wish I could remember more, but right now I can't. [Interviewer inquires.] Always a woman. It's always sex for drugs. Never gets to anything. I give her drugs, I use the drugs, I get paranoid and sick to my stomach. I feel in the dream like I do on cocaine. I don't have sex in the dream with these women. I always have a relationship with another woman, but one who doesn't use, and I never have sex with these women. [Later.] They are hookers. [Why hookers?] Not a big part of my life. [Hooked on drugs?] I don't know. [The women want drugs and are willing to give sex for drugs. You're sort of doing business then.] But I always had a relationship. I never used drugs with women I had a real relationship with.

His dreams always involved women, almost always prostitutes. He explained that he needed the hookers for the apparatus to take cocaine. Drug abuse almost always took place with hookers and always when he had another relationship with a woman. He never used cocaine with a woman with whom he had a relationship. He never has sex with the women, either in the dream or in waking life, because when he gets cocaine, he does not want sex. He explained that he only needed the equipment that the hookers could provide. He always awakened feeling the physiologic concomitants of craving and despair and horror that his life course had become hopeless ever since beginning cocaine seven years earlier. He feared that he would never change.

Commenting on the hookers, he said, "I got to know a lot of them. They had the apparatus to smoke cocaine. It wasn't sexual things. They don't want sex. They just want the drug. I'm really an outsider to the street life. I'm really very straight."

He described another nightmare:

Nightmare 2. I was a small child, about six or seven years old. It was in my home, and my mother and aunt were fighting, and I was trying to stop them. I don't know why they were fighting, but I loved them both and didn't want to see one hurt the other.

Then he commented, "Something like it happened, but I was older. I was 11."

The patient had a brother, 37, and a sister, 20. He never knew his biologic father. He was raised by his mother and his aunt. He recalled, to his horror, a time when his mother left the city. Only at the last moment was he was told of her leaving. He could still relive the terror. His aunt was a kindly woman, but his mother had beat him. The only person he was ever close to was his older brother, from whom he was now alienated because the patient had deceived and cheated him while involved with drugs. He felt that his brother had been favored by his mother. She would force the patient to stay home, to miss practice—he was very involved in sports—and would berate him and physically abuse him. As he talked, he became bitter and tearful about the damage this upbringing had wrought on his adult life. The quarrels between mother and aunt began when he was 11. When he was 13, his mother married a man who was an alcoholic and brutalized the mother. The patient once got in a physical fight with him at the age of 15.

He was a bright, reflective man who had finished high school and had a year of college. He entered military service at the age of 21, finished his tour of duty, and left the military. He had had a history of regular employment until a few years previously, when he apparently left jobs, for inexplicable reasons, but was not fired. He had relationships with women but, by his own admission, let nobody get close to him. He was a loner, now alienated from his entire family. This he blamed on himself because of his behavior when using drugs.

He was lost in bitterness and regrets about the course of his life and about what had happened to him during his early years. As he talked, he became tearful.

He described his dreams as typical of the withdrawal period for a week or so while he was crashing. He always had dreams of the prostitutes or of his mother and aunt quarreling.

His slip dreams—Nightmare 1 replays a situation in which he has control over women who need him for drugs, to whom he is not emotionally tied, and from whom he does not want sex. Nightmare 2 makes him younger, and hence more vulnerable, trying to stop the fight between his mother and his aunt. The younger age underscores his terror and lack of control over these women, fears that found their way into his adult attachment behaviors (and his escape from them in the scenario of the first dream). "Slipping" for him meant not merely relapse into drug use, but also the reentering of an exploitative world of control over women and their desires and over his feelings of attachment and vulnerabilities to loss and abandonment.

Case 6

A 37-year-old, recently divorced man readmitted for a variety of problems including schizophrenia, marital problems, and opiate and cocaine abuse, described a recent nightmare.

> *Nightmare 1.* It seemed very real. I was surrounded by a bunch of people that wanted to kill me and chopped my hands off. Then I woke up just before they got me. (6-1)

The patient explained that he had had this nightmare repetitively and that it usually accompanied conscious suicidal wishes when he felt like a failure. He described also both slip dreams and overdose dreams, actually nightmares. A "using" nightmare:

> *Nightmare 2.* I run into people I used to know, people on the street. Before I know it, I'm using again. That is when I woke up. [In response to question] I felt anxious. [Question about whether these dreams predicted relapse] Usually not, but this time I did. I did have the dream and the relapse, but usually I don't. Before I came in the hospital, I had these every night. [After questioning] No women in the dream. Didn't know the people. Not members of my family. Usually people with whom I used.

An "overdose" nightmare:

Nightmare 3. I start using heroin again. I overdose. I'm by myself or with Ron, a friend who uses. Usually I wake up before I die. I usually don't use after a dream like that.

These dreams seem to be warnings he listened to, as though his conscience were saying, Watch it; this could happen. Overdose dreams are usually connected with resisting the temptation to use. He had both the using and the overdose dreams when in withdrawal, and the nightmare the night before admission when he was consciously suicidal. That is, he had these dreams at times of crisis of failure in all aspects of his life.

The patient felt that these dreams, especially the dreams of dying, were predictive. He made no obvious connection between that and his conscious suicidal wishes.

He avoided sleep for fear that he would have a nightmare. He said that he stayed awake as long as he could, drank coffee and, in the past, took amphetamines to stay awake because he was terrified, and remains terrified. of sinking into dream states.

He also reported flying dreams (Nightmare 4), which he said "are my way of getting away from anything that can hurt me. I think the using dreams are a punishment."

People in the dreams are never family members. Sometimes they were people he knew on the street and used drugs with.

This patient, recently divorced from his wife, had become estranged from his 18-year-old stepson and 16-year-old daughter. He blamed himself for his marital difficulties stemming from his being an addict, lazy, and impotent (probably secondary to drugs, both Methadone and Stelazine).

His early years were quite traumatic. He never knew his biologic father. He had a brother and two sisters. His stepfather, a truck driver, was frequently away from home. There was no alcoholism or drugs in the family, but there was continual physical, sexual, and emotional abuse. His mother and her parents beat him repeatedly, and he reported that his mother sucked his penis on numerous occasions from the time he was five until he ran away from home at the age of nine. He apparently was then picked up by his stepfather but later set out again on his own and stayed on a ranch with a friend and his family. He felt that nobody had ever sided with him and that the whole family was against him.

The patient had tried unsuccessfully to engage in 12-step programs, which helped for a while, but he never fully engaged.

At times when he was in withdrawal, he had the dreams of using and of dying discussed earlier.

This was, then, a chronically schizophrenic man on Methadone for heroin use who now abused cocaine, who was grossly sexually and physically abused as a child, and had a sleep phobia.

The paranoid nightmare (Nightmare 1) may be seen as the state of mind in which the using dream (Nightmare 2) took takes place. The overdose dream (Nightmare 3) was identified by the patient as a punishment. Both the using dream (Nightmare 2) and the flying dream (Nightmare 4) are dreams in which he escaped from the tortured realities of his life—by drug abuse or by flight.

These slip nightmares do not simply portray the patient as tempted to use and in the throes of impending relapse. Patient 4 had a slip dream after a rejection from a long-term drug treatment program and upon discovering that his estranged wife was not at home to receive him after his pass. Patient 5 had slip nightmares restoring a situation in which his control over women sexually and otherwise was enhanced by the drug-using situation. The chronically psychotic, sexually abused patient 6 had using dreams and flying dreams to escape his unbearable reality and overdose dreams which he saw as punishments. In each of these cases, the slip dreams were in the immediate context of fears and failures in functioning—in relationships especially—that were somewhat ameliorated in fantasy (albeit at great cost) in the slipped, that is, the relapsed scenario.

For all three of these patients, the slip nightmare, by revealing the unconscious wish to slip, not only registered temptation and risk of relapse, but also provided an imaginary experience of a relapse that reinforced the fear and embarrassment of using as though a relapse had taken place. These nightmares may also be seen as evidence of the workings of unconscious guilt and wishes for punishment and failure. Such a signal from the unconscious underscored to all three of these men—even patient 4, who slipped—the fragility of the project of continued abstinence and the need to stay in a recovery program.

III

The phenomena of sleep phobia, slip dreams, and nightmares are of clinical interest in the understanding, and, eventually, in the treatment, of substance abuse. These phenomena, however, have more general significance. It is likely that sleep phobias, or fear of sleep, exists in other clinical settings where the afflicted person does not attempt to deal with the phobia by substance abuse. Slip dreams, which are well recognized in 12-step programs and recovery circles, may be one of a larger variety of other cases of dreams reflecting self-sabotage or risk of treatment failure, perhaps presaged by dreams of treatment sabotage analogous to slip dreams.

These observations point to the dream as a useful mental product, not simply an artifact, an epiphenomenon, or a matter for intensive psychotherapy alone. These dreams are of use to the clinician as naturalist exploring the depths and specific mechanisms underlying clinical phenomenology. Slip dreams can be seen as harbingers of potential relapse, of resistance, of self-sabotage, of factors opposing the process of recovery; and sleep phobia evidences the dreamer's fear of the unconscious itself and of the upsurge of terrifying dreams (often felt to be inevitable and predictable but insurmountable emotional turbulence finding its way into the overall problem of substance abuse. In both clinical situations, the dreams are still the royal road to the unconscious, not just in the psychoanalytic situation but to clinicians exploring the natural history of any emotional disturbance.

PART V

TREATMENT

CHAPTER 10

Exploration of Nightmares in Hospital Treatment of Borderline Patients

[with Carol R. Bley]

For a group of borderline patients whom we have been treating, their nightmares have proven to be a surprising marker for and source of insight into early familial trauma. In this chapter, we describe how the investigation of these nightmares positively influenced the overall treatment of these patients. The patients were recently admitted to an inpatient unit where family-centered psychodynamic psychotherapy is strongly emphasized. We did not originally intend to examine the patients' nightmares as part of our therapeutic strategy; the usefulness of the nightmares was a serendipitous finding that resulted from our clinical participation in our systematic investigation of nightmares of a similar patient population. In-depth investigations of nightmare phenomena illuminated the immediate clinical crisis of many patients in the light of their predisposing early familial trauma to such a degree that each patient's entire history of meaningful relationships appeared in a more continuous perspective than either the patients or their therapists had previously attained.

The borderline patients—in sharp contrast to those in our study of nightmares in psychoses—almost invariably wanted to talk more about their nightmares and to replay the audiotaped research interviews in the presence of their therapists. Even those patients for whom the investigation was a disorganizing and upsetting experience believed that the nightmares revealed something central about their psychological organization and that investigating the nightmares held a promise of helping them achieve a heretofore elusive wholeness and integration.

INVESTIGATION OF NIGHTMARES

Our interest in nightmares arose from clinical exigency. In the context of a group of patients who were survivors of physical or sexual abuse, we noted that a striking number suffered chronically from nightmares. Of these, about one third suffered from chronic posttraumatic nightmares, usually associated with military combat. Pharmacotherapy, individualized in each case to the clinical situation, often fell far short of alleviating the nightmares.

Schizophrenic and manic–depressive patients showed psychotic processes in their nightmares, which, with rare exception, revealed little that was not already clinically evident. Borderline patients (diagnosed according to DSM-III criteria [American Psychiatric Press, 1980]) were, on the contrary, generally impressed—as were the investigators—that the nightmares gave a useful perspective on their entire psychological life, so that the current crisis could be seen in the light of predisposing (i.e., early familial) factors with a lifelong and powerful influence on subsequent attachment behavior. The vast majority of this sample of nightmare sufferers had a lifelong history of familial trauma and dysfunction that, in the case of the posttraumatic nightmare sufferers, could be viewed as a predisposition, making the impact of the traumatic situation stronger and more pervasive. The preliminary results of this study have been detailed in chapters 2 and 3.

The borderline patients were frequently impressed with the usefulness of the insights gleaned from the investigation of their nightmares. Many patients wanted to talk to us again, to listen to the taped interviews again, or to play the tapes for their therapist. We were also impressed with the usefulness of the insights, and the project began to evolve into a procedure that could be used as part of the ward's overall treatment plan (if a patient consented). Most borderline patients were willing—even eager—to have the nightmare material integrated into their treatment, despite the distress caused by having to acknowledge the significance of such overwhelming material.

Case Examples

Case 1

A 52-year-old man in intensive therapy for six years was electively hospitalized to deal with his suicidality, which developed as he anticipated a divorce petition by his wife. Separated from his wife for 15 years, he knew that she had been involved with other men, including one with whom she had been living for many years. Nonetheless, the patient maintained that he was as attached as ever to her and was devastated by the prospect of divorce.

For several years, the patient's wife had held in check her desire for a divorce because of the patient's intimidating references to suicide. For example, he would say, "If you quit, then I'll quit." He was admitted to the hospital in part to help him through the difficult period when the divorce papers would be served, but also to address his need to intimidate and control his wife with threats of suicide. She was vulnerable to such intimidation because, several years earlier, when she had resumed her relationship with the patient after having been separated from him, her most recent boyfriend had committed suicide.

The patient reported that the night before admission, he had had— yet again—the following recurrent nightmare:

> I was on a ceiling looking down. There was a round bed. Z was on it. She was nude. There were chairs and there were men in them, nude. She had sex with each of them, first with one, then with another. I was upset. I wanted to scream, but I couldn't. I felt angry and upset, like it was punishment. I awoke. I felt relieved and then I felt depressed.

He had also experienced recurrent anxiety dreams about his wife, one of which was as follows:

> I took my wife out to dinner. We ate and talked. Then we went next door to a bar. She flirted with a guy at the bar. She left with him. I didn't feel much like a man.

The patient noted that he could anticipate having a nightmare whenever he thought about his wife. When she was on his mind, he tried to avoid nightmares by staying up late.

He had had an extraordinarily traumatic childhood. He was the only boy of six siblings. The closest person to him was a sister who died of diabetes at a young age. His parents' chaotic marriage was dominated by fights about the mother's overt infidelities. She often left the children at the movies during her trysts. She took the patient to movies where he was approached by homosexuals and repeatedly forced into homosexual activities. When he was seven, his parents divorced, and the courts refused to let either parent retain custody of the children. For the next seven years, his parents rarely saw him. He and his siblings were placed in orphanages and in foster homes for years, where the patient suffered further physical and sexual abuse.

He recalled that his nightmares began when he was seven. At first, he saw no connection between the nightmares and his mother's extramarital sexual activity, his own homosexual contacts, and his parents' divorce. He recalled a nightmare from childhood:

> I'm atop a stick, like on a telephone pole. The ground is covered with snakes. They're after me. I have to keep hopping, like on a pogo stick, to keep from being bitten.

He seemed surprised to pinpoint the date of this nightmare to a time when he was both aware of his mother's numerous lovers and himself involved in forced homosexual activity. He remembered another childhood nightmare:

> It was like levitation. I'm flying, looking down into a crowd of people who're after me.

The interviewer noted that the patient's dreams seemed to place him at a distance from events he could view from above. The patient said that he experienced the dreams as punishment and that he wanted to scream but could not. He found himself angry in the dreams and usually awoke tremendously relieved, but also feeling frightened and sinking into a predictable and inevitable depression. He seemed quite amazed when the interviewer connected the childhood nightmare involving snakes to his mother's trysts and his homosexual activity.

He recalled that for much of his young life he had thought that he was homosexual. Indeed, his intense attachment to his wife, signified by their marriage, reassured him that he would not deteriorate into a life of homosexual promiscuity. These fears of dissolution and deterioration had pushed him into the relationship with his wife, but only after six years of turbulent and intensive psychotherapy had he been able to tell his therapist some details of that homosexual activity. His clinical course during the past 10 years had been one of extreme depression, with numerous suicide attempts until he began intensive psychotherapy. In the course of this psychotherapy, his suicidal episodes were confined to ideation and treated with brief hospitalization. To his horror, about five years earlier, he had been diagnosed as having severe diabetes, which led him to recall with intense bitterness the loss of his sister, a brittle diabetic, who had died when she was very young. At times, in the midst of his depressive episodes when he became spitefully suicidal, he would stop taking insulin or would deliberately eat sugary foods to provoke a diabetic crisis. A side effect of his diabetes was impotence, which had affected him for the past four years.

In the course of interviewing the patient, the clinician conjectured that the person observed as the wife in the recurrent nightmare might represent not only the patient's wife, with whom the dream was manifestly concerned, but also his mother, with whom he now lived. And, of course, the person in the bed also represented the patient's worst fears about himself, that is, deterioration into homosexual promiscuity, a fate from which he himself acknowledged that his marriage had saved him, however precariously.

His recurrent nightmare gave the interviewers an unfolding sense of why his attachment to his wife, despite 15 years of separation and her long-term involvement with another man, retained such a tenacious hold on the patient. His desperation over the deteriorating relationship with her screened more terrifying and upsetting aspects of both his maternal object representation and his own self-representation. This overdetermination is revealed in the nightmare, which allowed expression of his anxiety about promiscuity while defending against an unmanageably upsetting awareness of his reaction to his mother's promiscuity and his own potential for promiscuous homosexuality. Also prominent in the series of dreams is a regression to voyeurism as a method of dealing with overwhelming castration anxiety.

With this understanding, the patient's desperate agenda of preventing his wife from officially divorcing him made more sense. Viewing his wife's promiscuity in recent nightmares screened his being upset both about his mother and about himself, exactly as had his original attachment to his wife. His current need to hold on to her (and to control her sadistically with threats of suicide) also served to contain his fear of regression to an amorphously perverse homosexual existence. (The snakes in the childhood dream attest to this unconscious fear.)

The fact that the patient could predict when he would have a nightmare (viz., when he was thinking about his wife) suggests that his anxiety and anger generated the nightmare and not that the nightmare generated the emotional turbulence. Following the nightmare, the patient experienced relief, a sense of the nightmare scenario as punishment, and inevitable depression. In fact, in the course of the interview, the patient correctly predicted that he would again have a nightmare and would feel worse because these upsetting issues had been brought to consciousness. The nightmares did, however, aid therapeutic focus, both on the continuity of his experience of attachment to unreliable (promiscuous) women, and on the fact that his excessive attachment to his estranged wife served to screen fears of his own homosexual tendencies.

Case 2

A 35-year-old married man was admitted to the hospital after a heavy bout of drinking during the previous month. His wife had suddenly quit her job, which left him with the entire financial responsibility for their family. The couple had been married only four years but had had four children before they married. Although he initially identified drinking as his only problem, he later came to understand that his drinking was, in some measure, a reaction that replaced expectable anger at his wife's neglect, lack of compassion for him as a breadwinner, and abdication of responsibility for the family's financial plight. He would rather drink than argue, and at first he found it difficult to think that he was angry with her at all. Yet he refused to clean the house as he had done before his wife stopped working.

His early upbringing was traumatic. One of seven children, he was his mother's help and consolation during the frequent absences of his father, a career military man whom the mother often derogated. The patient's siblings were treated like children (they were taken to movies, the zoo, and amusement parks), but he was not. His mother complained about her hard lot and criticized the father in confidence to the patient. While in school, the patient had numerous jobs and turned over all his earnings to his mother. He was also emotionally close to his maternal uncles, both of whom were alcoholics.

Mr. B recalled a nightmare:

> I wasn't at home. There was a knock at the door. Nobody answered. There was a person at the door who tried to force himself in. My wife and kids were there; so was my sister-in-law. There was another knock. I answer the door. (Surprise.) I struggle with the man. I said, "I'll call 911." My wife and kids and her sister were in the bedroom. The kids were running all around the house. The radio was blasting. I called 911 and reported the incident. When I gave them the description of the intruder, the description was of me. [Surprise.] Was I the one? There was another knock. The police came. They said, "Turn the music down." Every time they'd turn it down, it'd go up. The officer said, "Maybe we can unplug it." The stereo was by the fish bowl. The officer was electrocuted when he put his hand into the bowl. He yelled. I grabbed his hand; it was burned.

It was my hand. [Surprise.] I woke up. It was 3:30 a.m. I told the staff I just couldn't sleep.

The discussion of this nightmare evoked a recent newspaper story about a man who had killed his estranged wife, even though she had called for help to the emergency number 911. The interviewer suggested to the patient that the intruder may have represented a part of himself that was angry at his wife. The patient reacted with disbelief, but agreed that the evidence seemed convincing and left the interview in great perplexity.

In an interview the next day, he began to feel angry at his wife; he was able to acknowledge the anger for the first time but became extremely upset that he was angry at all. He had also become upset and tearful after being "disrespected" by another patient on the ward. His emotional balance was extremely labile and was characterized by tearfulness, proneness to feeling humiliated, and rage. Furthermore, he could not tolerate the idea of himself as an angry person. This young man was generally a straightforward, rather attractive, but fearful person who obviously wanted help and turned both to patients and to staff for further insights. He considered every comment from staff members with great seriousness.

The interview about the nightmare was disruptive for this patient because it brought back an unintegrated, angry part of himself that was disorganized, prone to shame, and filled with intolerable affect. He could appreciate that the intruder in the nightmare might represent an angry part of himself, but at this point he could not link the dream to his rage and attack on—but also his identification with—his absent and hated father, which was so clear from his childhood situation.

The nightmare helped the therapist focus on the patient's need to split off angry parts of himself and experience the anger as emanating from a source against which he could struggle. The patient's inability to tolerate being angry was only one aspect of a larger picture of affect intolerance that impeded his use of affect as a signal to help him deal with his interpersonal difficulties rather than turn to alcohol to obliterate the affect associated with them.

DISCUSSION

These cases illustrate how nightmares provided information that was useful in the overall treatment of borderline patients. The nightmares were studied in an investigation that began largely in isolation from the treatment effort, using only the limited associative material produced within an open-ended interview. Accordingly, the therapeutic work should be seen as a use of manifest content, limited associations, and latent content outside the context of intensive psychotherapy proper. This therapeutic work with nightmares, although far short of being fully interpretive, gave the investigators and the patients alike an enhanced appreciation of the significance of major life experiences screened by nightmares.

These nightmares were coherent dreams, not the poorly remembered dream fragments often found in the intensive psychotherapy of borderline patients. They had clear-cut latent content, and the disguise and dream work were identifiable, significant indicators of the patient's ego functioning. These nightmares, like those of most borderline patients in our sample, revealed no evidence of psychotic processes, that is, splits, blurring of self- and object boundaries, or ego disorganization. (The nightmares of the psychotic patients in our sample clearly showed these phenomena.) The absence of such features, which are often considered typical of the "object world" of borderline patients, was surprising, especially because these severely disturbed, hospitalized patients had been carefully diagnosed, meeting both psychoanalytic (Kernberg, 1984) and descriptive (American Psychiatric Association, 1980) criteria for borderline personality disorder. Our clinical material fails to support the notion that "borderline" patients should have "borderline" dreams or nightmares.

The nightmares dealt with familial trauma. Although they were not "replays" of actual traumatic events, they were clearly related to a current familial crisis that was intimately tied to the reason for the patient's hospitalization (Lansky, 1988, 1989). The nightmares in the two illustrative cases also had clear resonances with early familial trauma, although neither patient initially connected the nightmare to trauma in the family of origin.

Our working definition of nightmares as dreams accompanied by sufficient anxiety to awaken the dreamer was in accord with the definition elicited from virtually all our patients during interviews with them. We saw no reason to qualify the definition further.

The scope of this chapter allows for only brief discussion of pertinent literature. Freud (1900), challenging the notion that anxiety dreams contradicted the wish-fulfillment theory, noted that the anxiety accompanying such dreams must be understood from the point of view of the latent, not the manifest, content of the dream. Accordingly, anxiety dreams proved problematic regarding the source of the anxiety, rather than concerning the (sleep-preserving, anxiety-lowering) function of dreams per se. The case involving posttraumatic anxiety dreams was more problematic because posttraumatic nightmares have been perceived as "replays" of the trauma and, hence, without latent content or dream work. Freud (1920) postulated a wish *from the ego* (i.e., the wish for mastery) in the traumatic neuroses. The attempt, exemplified in the posttraumatic nightmare, was to master the overwhelming stimulus retrospectively by developing anticipatory anxiety, the absence of which had been an etiological factor in the traumatic neurosis.

In a major synthesis of developmental, laboratory, and ego-psychological findings, Mack (1970) expanded our understanding of nightmares to include the revival of early ego states of helplessness, the fear of aggression and its consequences (i.e., annihilation or loss of need-satisfying objects), and the distortions resulting specifically from ego defenses against aggression. Mack recognized a major adaptive aspect to nightmares but concluded that nightmares cannot be seen as either completely adaptive or completely symptomatic.

The only available literature on the therapeutic use of nightmares concerned posttraumatic nightmares, where manifest content was viewed as a simple replay of the traumatic event and the therapy attempted to integrate the overwhelming experience into the patient's mental life (Blitz and Greenberg, 1984). Latent content and dream work were assumed either to be absent from or irrelevant to the therapeutic use of the nightmare.

Dreams that surface during the intensive psychotherapy of borderline patients have been regarded as problematic. Green (1977) viewed them as primarily evacuative and reflective of the dreamer's wish to dispose of an aspect of the self-representation that is unacceptable in patients whose personality is organized around splitting rather than around repression (Bion, 1977; Segal, 1981).

Oremland (1987) has noted that conflict in the dreams of borderline patients reflects a decidedly different level of self-object differentiation from conflict in dreams of either neurotic or narcissistic patients or of schizophrenic patients. The former have clear-cut self-object differentiation, while the latter have a fusion of self- and object boundaries.

Self psychologists, beginning with Kohut (1977), have noted dreams whose meaning is not clarified even when the patient produces detailed associations. These dreams, which have been likened to traumatic dreams (Grinstein, 1983), portray the incohesive ego in a state of impending fragmentation; they are referred to as "self-state dreams" (Kohut, 1977; Ornstein, 1987; Reed, 1987; Slap and Trunnell, 1987).

In our study of nightmares produced by recently hospitalized borderline patients, we did not find these perspectives useful. In the two illustrative cases, the nightmare texts of both patients revealed unacceptable aspects of the self that were projected onto other persons. In the first patient's dream, the patient's wife carried disowned or repressed sexual propensities belonging to the patient's maternal object representation as well as to his own self-representation. In the second patient's dream, the assailant and the police officer represented aspects of the patient's self. In both cases, "displacement" and "condensation," standard terminology of dream work, seemed more useful than "evacuation." That is to say, unacceptable parts of the self were not simply gotten rid of; they were relocated. The dreams did not strike us as showing clear-cut evidence of blurring or fusing of self- and object boundaries. Nor was the term "self-state dreams" appropriate for these nightmares: the meaning of the dream deepened with more associative material, and fragmentation or ego disorganization was not the major issue dealt with in the dreams.

Conclusions concerning our findings are, of course, somewhat tentative because our material does not arise entirely from the associative method in the context of ongoing intensive psychotherapy. It was nonetheless a striking and somewhat unexpected finding that therapeutic attention to these nightmares, despite the added disruption resulting from the erosion of their screening function, proved as fruitful to the treatment effort as does interpretation of dreams in the intensive psychotherapy of neurotic patients. These nightmares enabled investigators, therapists, and patients to view a patient's life as a coherent, continuous whole in the focused and synthetic fashion expectable in any form of intensive psychotherapy involving dream interpretation. They proved a royal—if somewhat rocky—road to a knowledge of the unconscious.

In noting the usefulness of integrating results of our study of nightmares with an entire treatment effort for hospitalized borderline patients, we must firmly caution against the therapeutic use of nightmares outside the present treatment context, that is, a treatment setting characterized by (1) a supportive holding environment, (2) considerable experience in the treatment of borderline patients, (3) familiarity with an intergenerational familial perspective, and (4) disciplined use of psychodynamic dream interpretation.

CHAPTER 11

Treatment Considerations

THE NEED FOR A MODEL

Nightmares have long been appreciated as an emblematic feature of the posttraumatic clinical picture. Most prevailing schools of thought, whether dynamic, behavioral, or biologic, have viewed the posttraumatic nightmare as replaying the very essence of what is traumatic about the traumatic event. That is to say, they see the manifest content of the nightmare as essentially a visual replay of the trauma and the traumatic conflict.

It is easy, even compellingly intuitive, to so privilege the manifest content of the trauma. Therapeutic views that lay such exclusive emphasis on the manifest content implicitly or explicitly constitute interpretations as to the meaning of that trauma or its significance. Freud (1920, 1933) himself presumed without serious empirical inquiry that the manifest content of repetitive posttraumatic nightmares portrayed the essence of the trauma, so much so that there was no latent content, no dream work, and only a wish to master the trauma by reexperiencing it with anticipatory anxiety (Freud, 1920).

A variant of the same point of view from a self psychological perspective regards the traumatic situation solely in terms of the experience of the event encapsulated in the nightmare scenario. The terrifying episode, so disturbing that it has become split off as an unintegrated traumatic preoccupation, must be empathically reexperienced to be integrated within the mainstream of psychic life.

161

Much the same exclusive emphasis underlies behavioral or implosive techniques that deploy forced reliving of the scenario by implosion as the therapeutic centerpiece.

These points of view share a basic model of traumatic impact, made explicit in chapter 1, which serves as the basis for psychotherapeutic strategies of any kind. The assumptions are that 1) the nightmare portrays the essence of what is traumatic about the trauma; (2) the nightmare has no latent content that is of significance—that is to say, that the nightmare is more like an affectively charged memory than a true dream; (3) accordingly, that the manifest content is not a product of transformations of the dream work serving defensive functions or portraying wishes as fulfilled; (4) therefore, the conflict represented in the nightmare scenario, usually one over fear of external danger occasionally with conscious remorse, is the central or only conflict to be addressed in the therapy; and (5) the nightmare is itself part of the stress response reaction, as inflammation is to injury of physical tissue, and is (somehow) driven into existence by the trauma that is represented in the manifest content of the nightmare.

On the basis of the extensive clinical studies presented earlier in this book, I contend that all the assumptions of this basic model are false and that the adoption of such an oversimplified model puts forward a *pars pro toto* view of the pathological predicament posed by posttraumatic nightmares. These assumptions, taken together, form a constricted view of the nightmare that seriously compromises the psychotherapeutic enterprise by ignoring predisposing, coexisting, and contemporaneous narcissistic traumata, all of which involve conflicts posed by psychic disorganization and shame that resonate with, and are evoked by, shame and disorganization in the posttraumatic state that are screened by the manifest content of the posttraumatic nightmare. Conflicts involving unconscious guilt are also ignored.

This challenge to the implicit basic model common to many approaches to the trauma victim is not put forward with the intent of discrediting the significance of the manifest issues in the nightmare scenario. The intent, rather, is to view the impact of the manifest trauma in the posttraumatic state in the context of the victim's entire nexus of unconscious conflicts, meaningful psychic connections, and current interpersonal circumstances so as to evolve a model better suited to the treatment of a wider variety of cases.

The preceding chapters have explored the dynamic significance of nightmares in a sample of deeply disturbed patients observed and treated in a hospital setting. It cannot be assumed, of course, for posttraumatic nightmares generally, or any one nightmare sufferer in particular, that all posttraumatic nightmare sufferers have significant preexisting psychopathology, much less psychopathology of the magnitude experienced by the patients in these studies. The extent to which the results of these studies can be generalized to less severely disturbed populations, therefore, must remain open to fresh reappraisal from case to case.

The reader who assumes that the material in chapters 2 through 10 applies only to that portion of the clinical population confined to severely disturbed patients risks dismissing application of the more general principles garnered from these studies to the problem of posttraumatic nightmares generally. The whole question of the relationship of nightmare to pathology—that is, of the traumatic impact of outer danger on previously disturbed inner experience—cannot be avoided without greatly oversimplifying our understanding of the clinical field in which posttraumatic nightmares, especially delayed, intermittent, or chronic ones, arise.

What follows is an attempt to replace the inexplicit model of traumatic impact currently prevalent with an explicit and more encompassing one that takes both relatively simple and more complicated cases into account. The first step in the evolution of such a model is a conceptualization of the posttraumatic state that provides the backdrop against which relatively uncomplicated posttraumatic reactions as well as those complicated by preexisting psychopathology can be understood. Although detailed examination of the psychotherapy of the traumatized patient is beyond the purview of this book, I shall offer a preliminary conceptualization of the way in which a model of posttraumatic psychopathology and a dynamic understanding of posttraumatic nightmares fit into the psychotherapeutic situation.

THE POSTTRAUMATIC STATE

Without presupposing the presence of preexisting psychopathology in the trauma victim, one may start with the assumption that a posttraumatic state occurs in anyone in reaction to trauma of significant magnitude. This posttraumatic state is the background disturbance in the light of which the posttraumatic nightmare can be seen as an attempt at repair.

Features of the relatively uncomplicated posttraumatic state include (but are not limited to) an increase in vulnerability and in requirements for environmental responsiveness. In cases of trauma that result from frank human malevolence or attack, there is added symptomatology reactive to that malevolence per se.

The posttraumatic state is one in which the sense of self is fractured. There is a greater or lesser degree of disorganization of the personality, fragmentation, decreased cohesion, and dissociation—a fluidly altered psychic state that may be either very transient or very enduring, and that may change in steady state with perceived danger in the immediate environment.

This posttraumatic state is usually accompanied by a dramatic increase of needs that result from this vulnerability—needs for a more attuned or responsive human environment to provide conditions of safety, support, and affirmation. This increased need of others, together with (what may be more visible) reactions against such needs, amplifies, of course, every preexisting conflict associated with dependent relationships or with dependency itself, especially as the trauma victim sees himself or herself as more than usually dependent for security on the responsiveness of others. One finds, therefore, combinations of amplified awareness of the need for the social bond and reactions against such an awareness. This is manifest as either a pronounced increase in neediness or a pronounced withdrawal from social interactions; that is to say, an increased reliance on the supportive social bond or increased embarrassment about the loss of self-sufficiency that gives rise to a need for increased social bonding. Since shame is the emotion that signals danger to the social bond (Scheff, 1990), shame conflicts in particular are activated by the posttraumatic state.

If the trauma had to do with human malevolence—for example, attack, rape, sexual abuse, concentration camp internment—then the posttraumatic state will be further complicated by a loss of confidence in work, home, relationships, and so forth, which provide a containing function and give the sense of a familiar environment that is basically trustworthy. The loss of such a sense of confidence becomes a source of active feelings of estrangement, fear, and disorganization. The trauma victim is aware of the loss of the (perhaps illusory) feeling of familiarity and safety of the environment. That loss is accompanied by a sense of shame that comes from the realization that one is not the way other people are and that also comes from the risk of public exposure as someone who is mistrustful, frightened, and alarmed when other people are not. This upsurge of shame or of shame anxiety is often handled by global withdrawal or outright hiding.

If the trauma results from specifically *human* malevolence, (e. g., rape, combat, mugging, abuse), the victim may also react with tendencies to identify with the aggressor (A. Freud, 1937)—that is, to become in unconscious fantasy identified with the frightening malefactor and to project the aggression on a victim who receives traumatic injury in the same way that the sufferer did. This identification with the aggressor, or turning of the tables, is a method of handling shame by reversal, but it is also a mechanism that generates still more shame if the former victim's aggression gets out of control, along with considerable guilt resulting from the real or fantasied consequences of aggression.

It should be noted that the shame attendant to trauma, while often symptomatic, is not necessarily pathological if it arises from modification in the awareness of the self before others—that is, of himself or herself as more than previously in need of responsiveness, more frightened of the environment, more fragile internally, and even as one who has, to some extent, internalized aspects of the trauma that in turn give rise to subsequent intrapsychic conflict.

THE POSTTRAUMATIC STATE AND FAILURE OF ENVIRONMENTAL RESPONSIVENESS

I turn now to a discussion of the consequences of shame generated by a relative failure of the environment in the face of the changes in the sense of self, the need for others, and the experience of the environment brought about by the posttraumatic state. The important role of guilt is also discussed.

The increased neediness for others to provide a stable, affirmative, and responsive environment; fear of the environment itself; and internalization of certain aspects of the traumatic experience unite to create an imbalance between need and environmental responsiveness. In the absence of sufficient responsiveness, symptomatology will arise. This is not an indication of preexisting psychopathology per se, although the traumatized victim may be highly symptomatic for some time, even indefinitely under unfavorable circumstances, which include strength of trauma, hostility of the environment, preexisting pathology, and lack of responsiveness of the support system. Posttraumatic symptoms, then, derive from some combination of strength of the trauma and failure of the environment to respond sufficiently to the trauma sufferer when in a vulnerable posttraumatic state.

All the features of the posttraumatic state are potentially shame generating. Put simply, the victim is humiliated by the exposure of needs, especially in the presence of unresponsiveness or rejecting responses from others in the environment or aspects of the self (for example, unconscious homosexual conflicts) that may come to awareness when the patient's neediness pushes him or her into an unusual reliance on other persons.

Many victims, as we noted in the previous section, handle the shame by an identification with the aggressor. One can see this identification basically as a defense against shame by such a fantasied turning of the tables. But the consequent loss of control of aggressiveness generates even more shame, and the real or fantasied destructive consequences of the rage generate guilt so that a vicious cycle is activated.

Unacknowledged shame, as Lewis (1971) has so persuasively pointed out, leads to rage; owing to the masking properties of this rage, the shame attendant to the posttraumatic situation may remain unacknowledged and hence escalate to symptomatic proportions. The shame results from exposure of loss of control, loss of composure, loss of integrity, and loss of poise. Although she does not use the term specifically, Lewis is referring to narcissistic rage. Her studies point to the likelihood that a shame experience, conscious or unconscious, preceded an episode of rage. The rage itself gives rise to guilt about the consequences of rage or of destructive attack.

Shame also gives rise to defenses against the increased experience of shame. The shame-filled posttraumatic patient may experience fear, depression, and, above all, constriction of social activity. Constriction of activity to the point of total isolation is clinically one of the underrecognized major signs in posttraumatic states; it applies to combat veterans, rape victims, Holocaust survivors, and many other trauma victims, especially if the trauma in question is due to human malevolence. The reactions to shame may also show up in a fear of both intimacy and abandonment and a rigidification in the trauma victim's requirements for optimal distance from others. For the shame-filled person, both intimacy and separation are ever present dangers.

ACTIVATION OF PREEXISTING SHAME CONFLICTS

The symptomatic state of affairs described in the preceding section may result solely from external trauma in combination with environmental unresponsiveness in the absence of preexisting or coexisting psychopathology. To the extent that preexisting psychopathology is evoked or activated by the posttraumatic state, the clinical picture becomes more complicated: the trauma becomes processed unconsciously as a continuation of these preexisting issues. The cases in chapters 2 through 10 are at this level of clinical complexity.

Shame conflicts are emphasized here not because they occur to the exclusion of guilt conflicts or because they are presumed to be, in every case, more important; but because they pertain more immediately to the sense of self before others that is fractured in any posttraumatic state and because it is in the nature of shame and shame conflicts to remain masked or hidden. Shame-related issues are therefore likely to be missed in the therapeutic situation unless they are actively looked for.

Awareness of the ubiquity and clinical centrality of posttraumatic states and their attendant feelings of neediness and shame should help point both the therapist and the dreamer in the direction of the current day material that instigated the posttraumatic nightmare.

The posttraumatic state as a source of shame may resonate with preexisting shame conflicts in a number of ways: shame may result from an increase in panic, loss of composure, hypersexuality, aggression, all of which generate shame over the loss of control and activate similar conflicts. In reaction to this loss of control, there may be actual or feared exposure before others, criticism, or rejection by others, the net result of which is disorganization and even more shame. If that shame is unacknowledged, it may culminate in narcissistic rage and consequent vengefulness, irresponsibly demanding behaviors, or withdrawal. There may also be activation of anticipated responses from others—rejection, withdrawal, retaliation—that have been associated with prior and coexisting conflicts.

Preexisting shame from another source may become part of the escalation of trauma instigated by a posttraumatic state. Such preexisting shame may come from childhood conflicts in which the future trauma victim was overtly shamed or felt exposed as weak, selfish, unlovable; identification with a parent held in contempt, particularly the same-sex parent; shame over the workings of guilt or self-sabotage (see cases 1 and 3 of rape victims discussed in chapter 8); any state of neediness or excessive reliance on dyads resulting from preexisting childhood trauma; homosexual conflicts resulting from identification with aspects of acts of violence or exposure to violence; and any of the sequelae discussed earlier having to do with the mechanism of identification with the aggressor.

All such potential shame conflicts from narcissistic trauma and character pathology can be activated by the posttraumatic state and relative failure of the environment. The full blown clinical pictures presented in the preceding chapters illustrate the escalation of these conflicts. (See chapter 6 for an example of shame due to homosexual conflict and chapter 8, Case 3, for an example of shame accompanying humiliating discrediting in a rape victim.)

THE ROLE OF GUILT

Guilt plays an important role in the posttraumatic picture in all trauma sufferers. It is, of course, important to distinguish *conscious guilt* or remorse, which appears as an affect, from *unconscious guilt,* which may show up as a feeling of unworthiness or badness or which may be inferred from repeated self-defeating, self-punishing, or self-sabotaging actions or from reckless exposure to retraumatization.

Guilt is less an immediate reaction to the vulnerable posttraumatic state per se than shame, but it is nonetheless a significant factor in every posttraumatic reaction. Guilt may enter the clinical picture in a number of quite different ways, which they are of different psychodynamic and psychotherapeutic significance:

1. Preexisting guilt may be a factor in repeated and apparently unheeding exposure to the risk of trauma. If unconscious guilt is involved in the exposure to traumatic risk, such exposure is a sign of severe characterologic or neurotic disturbance. The phenomena described here are indicated in the "criminals from the sense of guilt" that Freud (1916a), following Nietzsche (1888), described. Lidz (1946) found that combat soldiers with the worst nightmares were those who had a conscious hatred of their fathers and rage generating guilt of suicidal proportions. Lidz concluded that the dream scene may be seen as fulfilling a suicidal wish. The same may be said of many other nightmares that portray the results of rage and destructiveness. In some cases, this is identification with the aggressor; in many others, it reflects the shame/rage cycle that results from the humiliation caused by the trauma and its consequent rage. In these cases, the clinician should search for antecedent humiliating traumatic experiences that gave rise to either rage or identification with the aggressor and that, in either case, gave rise to guilt, generating the wish for punishment. The exposure to the trauma itself or the nightmare may thus be understood. It is, of course, never justifiable to evoke the concept of preexisting guilt to discredit the trauma victim.

2. A second type of guilt arises from the rageful affect and aggressive action that invariably follow the unacknowledged shame generated by the posttraumatic state. The connection between unacknowledged (often unconscious) shame and narcissistic rage has been elegantly demonstrated by Lewis (1971). I am adding here only the relationship between such shame/rage cycles and subsequent guilt, whether conscious or unconscious, resulting from that rage. The initial shame may come from an excessive neediness that results in compensatory manipulation or sadistic control of other persons—

that is to say, from what I have elsewhere called pathologic distance regulation (Lansky, 1992a). There may be guilt in response to out-pourings of narcissistic rage, hostile acting out on the basis of identification with the aggressor, or the irresponsible demandingness that results from a sense of entitlement. These latter dynamics typify Freud's (1916a) "exceptions," those who "want too much" (Kris, 1976), who feel that because of their hurts and the damage done to them the rules do not apply to them, that they are justified in making entitled demands or angry attacks.

3. Yet another source of guilt may derive from infantile omnipotence as it enters into one's attempt to deal with the state of helplessness following the trauma. The patient, by the voiced or merely felt attitude, "I set this up," "I deserve this," "This is all my fault," effects a fantasied transformation from the passive "It happened to me" to the active, but guilt-ridden, "I did it." Shameful helplessness in the face of the absence of order in the world is, so to speak, converted in fantasy into the more empowering guilty omnip-otence, the guilt being the price of a somewhat enhanced sense of self. For the person feeling guilty in the wake of trauma, there is a greater sense of responsibility, whatever the cost, and less of a sense of helplessness, randomness, and irrelevance—"It is because of my sexuality, my aggression" rather than "It is a matter of my power-lessness." These derivatives of infantile omnipotence are actually an aspect of secondary revision. Most of the sense of guilt in these situations does not have to do with actual harm done to others but with the endopsychic awareness of self-sabotage.

The relations among these sources of guilt are complex. A preex-isting conflict, in the face of which the patient feels guilty (chapter 8, Case 1), results in self-sabotage, which gives rise to shame, a sense that "I set this up; I don't deserve anything," and consequent self-condemnation. Guilt, then, fuels the self-sabotage and the exposure to the trauma that give rise to shame.

THE POSTTRAUMATIC NIGHTMARE IN RELATION TO THE POSTTRAUMATIC STATE AND ITS NEXUS OF CONNECTIONS

The Latent Content

The posttraumatic vulnerability, the expectations for environmental responsiveness, the shame and consequent rage and resultant guilt, and the nexus of reactivated, archaic, and current conflicts constitute the day residue of the posttraumatic nightmare. It is within this fluid, disorganized, posttraumatic state of narcissistic and affective imbalance, amplified by related past and current conflicts, that the latent content of the dream is to be found.

This conceptualization of the latent content is the more clinically significant because detailed psychotherapeutic exploration informed by a sensitivity to shame usually confirms Levin's (1967) observation that, whereas the experiences of guilt tend to push clinical material into awareness, shame experiences and shame conflicts tend to drive even significant clinical material out of the awareness of the patient and hence out of the purview of the psychotherapy session. The clinician aware of the ubiquity of such posttraumatic states will be better prepared to search for them and to recognize subtle signs of them and allusions to them. They are commonly reignited when an experience of disorganization and shame disconnects the trauma sufferer from a sense of attachment to the social order.

Instigation

The issue of instigation of posttraumatic nightmares is one that has been sidestepped by trauma researchers, by sleep laboratory investigators, and, curiously enough, by psychoanalysts beginning with Freud. For Freud (1920, 1933) posttraumatic nightmares were simple recapitulations of a traumatic event and had no dream work, latent content, defensive function, or instigation. The failure to look for instigating experiences is the more remarkable in view of Freud's (1900) sensitivity to shaming experiences in the day preceding his own dreams (Lansky and Morrison, in press).

An experience of shame, with its chain of reverberating effects, is often found to be the disturbance in the dream day that instigates the nightmare and constitutes its latent content. Guilt may be involved in trauma cases as a motive for increased risk of exposure to trauma, as a reaction to narcissistic rage arising from shame, or through the workings of secondary revision resulting from omnipotent afterthought. But it is the experience of narcissistic injury, shame, disorganization, and the escalation of shame that should be sought out as the major instigator of the posttraumatic nightmare. The clinician should be aware that a protracted or recurring fluid posttraumatic state is often an enduring part of the very acute posttraumatic picture; as such, it serves as a more or less steady source of instigation of repetitive nightmares in the acute stage of posttraumatic disturbance. An appreciation of such states will enhance the clinician's sensitivity to the fact that the patient risks more shame if exposed as vulnerable and needy. The clinician will be better able to help the patient talk about these issues in a therapeutic situation that minimizes the added upset that comes from a focus on shame.

The Dream Work

Evidence of dream work and transformation of affect are easier to appreciate once the therapist acquires a feel for the type of latent content and shame conflicts that are the ubiquitous accompaniments of the posttraumatic state and the trauma sufferer's defenses against exposure of shameful experiences. The dream work consists of the operations by which the manifest dream has come to represent sources of disruption in an attempt to minimize them.

In the preceding chapters, the operations of the dream work were clearly visible in comparing the patient's accounts of the traumatic scene with that same patient's account of the nightmare. The nightmare, in selecting from material in which the patient's self-representation is more or less intact, albeit in a situation of overwhelming danger, not only screens the narcissistic injury resulting from the trauma itself, but also represents and at the same time disguises a host of other narcissistic traumata that generate intense shame (Lidz, 1946). Narcissistic rage arising from unacknowledged shame and hostility from any other source gives rise to guilt. The repetition of the danger situation in the posttraumatic nightmare may also reflect the workings of unconscious guilt that is a consequence of that rage and results in the wish for punishment.

The screening function of the nightmare, by using the dream work to substitute an intact, albeit endangered, self in the manifest content of the nightmare for the fragmented and shame-filled self-experience of the dream day, also, in effect, transforms shame into fear (see chapter 5). Guilt is evidenced in the manifest nightmare, in which the sense of guilt has been transformed into fear of attack from without, and the wish for punishment is experienced concretely as a return to the traumatic situation.

Another aspect of the screening function of the dream work is the editing of the trauma for defensive purposes (chapter 8, Case 3). Here is screening not by discrepancy in the content of the manifest dream compared with trauma, but in the selection of one facet of the traumatic scenario over others to dramatize a point, for example, in the case just referred to, as a justification to dismissive authorities of the danger encountered by the patient.

In very acute posttraumatic states, especially those in which the trauma is a result of human malevolence, the dream work is particularly pointed toward *preparation to avoid retraumatization*. This was especially evident in the acute nightmares of recently raped women hospitalized in a mostly male ward (chapter 8; see also Weiss and Sampson, 1986).

Secondary revision (Freud, 1900 is commonly found in the dreamer's attitude toward the dream: "It was about the trauma"; "It was an exact repeat of what happened," even though the person's reports of the dream and the trauma differ significantly. The secondary revision gains a defensive function by removing any curiosity about the discrepancy in the dream scenario compared with the recollection of the trauma. The dream is filed in the patient's consciousness more or less as an affect-laden memory to be dismissed as a somewhat distant experience that is simply an "instant replay."

Another aspect of secondary revision portrayed in the patient's attitude toward the trauma reflects the workings of unconscious guilt; that is, the attitude that "I set this up"; "I deserved it." Even if there is some evidence for purposeful exposure to trauma (chapters 6 and 8), such self-condemnation reflects the workings of infantile omnipotence in the defensive conversion of the experience of passive (and shame filled) helplessness ("It was done to me") to active (albeit empowered) wrong-doing ("I did it"; "I set it up").

Wish Fulfillment

The wish-fulfillment hypothesis is the centerpiece of any psychodynamic appreciation of dreaming because of the overriding significance of seeing the dream as having not simply meaning but also *function.* The essence of a psychodynamic attitude toward dreams is an overarching view of the dream as instigated in response to a disturbance in psychic equilibrium and functioning, in an attempt at least, to deal with that disturbance. It was over the apparent failure of posttraumatic nightmares to fit into the theory of wish fulfillment that Freud (1920) postulated the instinct for mastery and the compulsion to repeat. These speculations were made in the absence of the clinical phenomenology that is so characteristic of Freud's other writing on dreams. I, of course, contend that posttraumatic nightmares do not pose exceptions to the wish-fulfillment hypothesis.

The manifest content of the dream, then, looked at in terms of *function,* can be seen as a solution to a problem that was posed by the disturbance, that is, the posttraumatic state. The manifest dream does so by creating an experience which may be seen as a fulfillment of a wish (Lansky, 1992b). In the case of posttraumatic nightmares, however disturbing, such wish fulfillment can be inferred from the activities of the dream work. To name those just mentioned: screening of shame-producing experiences in the day residue by fear-producing ones in the manifest content; screening of other narcissistic traumata; screening of the wish for punishment resulting from unconscious guilt; transformations of affects; editing of aspects of the traumatic scenario for defensive purposes; and various aspects of secondary revision.

It may perhaps be useful for the psychodynamic therapist to think not just abstractly about wish fulfillment in a theoretical sense but more specifically about the posttraumatic state and its nexus of connections as posing a disturbance; and of the posttraumatic nightmare, however distressing, as attempting, as it were, to do something about it. It is in this sense that wish fulfillment comes into play in any truly dynamic approach to the posttraumatic nightmare that does not oversimplify the clinical situation as simply a reflex response to the manifest trauma depicted in the nightmare.

THE PSYCHOTHERAPEUTIC SITUATION

All the foregoing psychodynamic considerations, from the simplest to the most complex, must be taken into account in the psychotherapy of posttraumatic patients.

The features of simple posttraumatic vulnerability and its heightened need for environmental responsiveness have an obvious significance for the therapeutic relationship, and the conflicts posed by such vulnerability and neediness find their way into the transference. On occasion, with simple, uncomplicated traumatic reactions, usually those that do not result from human malevolence—for example, auto accidents or natural disasters—a straightforward need for human responsiveness while in a heightened state of posttraumatic vulnerability can be met in a simple, supportive fashion that will enhance the natural healing process. But the existence of such uncomplicated cases does not justify extrapolating an oversimplified model to more complex clinical situations, especially if the trauma is a result of human malevolence. The assumption should never be made a priori that a posttraumatic clinical picture is a result of simple, traumatic impingement without complications from predisposing conflict and traumata.

The presence of posttraumatic nightmares, even in such uncomplicated cases, is an indication to investigate the fragile posttraumatic state that is instigating these nightmares. The nightmares themselves, in simple cases, usually remain consistent and repetitive and blend into other dream elements within six to eight weeks (Hartmann,

1984). These cases may not require nuanced psychodynamic handling.

In many posttraumatic reactions, however, and especially those due to malevolent trauma, the situation is more complex and the trauma should be viewed as something superimposed on a nexus of preexisting conflict (not always pathological) stirred up by the posttraumatic vulnerability and enhanced neediness of the trauma victim. The presence of nightmares together with daytime preoccupation with trauma combine with latent conflicts stirred up by the posttraumatic state to form what should, perhaps, be considered a *traumatic psychoneurosis*; this psychoneurosis is typically superimposed on underlying biologic posttraumatic vulnerabilities. Like any psychoneurosis, the superimposed posttraumatic psychoneurosis protects, but also retards the resolution and healing of, the underlying disturbance. Simplistic responses to such clinical situations and a narrow and literal reading of the significance of the trauma in the nightmare scenario is wrong-headed and inadequate to the clinical task at hand.

Chronic, delayed, or recurrent posttraumatic nightmares point to the recognition of a psychoneurotic aspect of the posttraumatic picture that, by weaving the traumatic situation into the texture of the dreamer's preexisting conflicts, is attempting to solve problems posed by the posttraumatic state in ways that compound the destructive effects of the trauma—that is to say, by screening out experiences associated with shame and guilt conflicts to the point that they hold the traumatic fixation in place and retard the course of healing.

The point of view put forward here specifically takes issue with treatment strategies that work either by flooding or by abreactive strategies directed toward the literal dream scenario only. I propose instead that the posttraumatic nightmare be used like any other dream in dynamic psychotherapy: as a true dream, having a manifest content that must be taken seriously, but also seen very much as a compromise formation. It follows that proper handling of the posttraumatic nightmare will include, but also go far beyond, the surface issue represented in the nightmare scenario. Any therapeutic strategy that privileges the manifest content to the point of excluding attention to the current posttraumatic state, the interpersonal conflicts that the state engenders, and the intrapsychic conflicts that the state reactivates (that is to say, the latent content which instigates the nightmare), basically colludes with the screening function of the posttraumatic nightmare and keeps the latent content concealed from therapeutic scrutiny. This focus sidesteps central difficulties that desperately need attention in the here and now of the dreamer's current reality. In particular, treatment strategies that privilege discussion of the traumatic scenario exclusively fail to use the posttraumatic nightmare to delve deeply enough to clarify crucial here-and-now issues in the life of the traumatized person that are masked, rationalized, or hidden from view because they give rise to shame or shame conflicts.

The dream work provides guidelines for exploration of these deeper issues since it points to the defensive operations that hold the traumatic fixation and the dreamer's response to it in place, thereby preventing the clarification and resolution of the psychoneurosis that covers over the basic traumatic disturbance. The issues underlying these defensive and synthetic operations of the dream work—the conflicts that generate the attempt at wish fulfillment—are, of course, likely to find their way into the therapeutic relationship in the form of conflicts that complicate the treatment alliance and the therapeutic work.

The studies discussed in chapters 2-10 are rich in details of dream formation and are clinically embedded. These studies, however, carried out in a setting in which only short term work was possible, do not extend to the domain of comprehensive psychotherapeutic management. They do not, that is, provide specific information on matters of special concern to the psychodynamic psychotherapist faced with the treatment of the trauma victim. I refer to special problems affecting the treatment alliance, the transference resistances, enactments, and termination in the psychotherapy of the posttraumatic patient (see, for example, Dewald, 1989; Terr, 1991; Herman, 1992).

The clinical material does, nonetheless, provide dramatic examples of enactments in the clinical setting that, viewed psychotherapeutically, are instances of acting out that sabotage or threaten to sabotage the treatment efforts and the course of recovery from trauma. As such, they are not only enactments; they also presage transference resistances that consciously or unconsciously oppose the treatment process.

Insofar as dreams, posttraumatic nightmares included, represent wishes as fulfilled, they provide a key to self-sabotaging, self-defeating, masochistic, and outright suicidal wishes that may subsequently be acted out (Roth, 1958; Segal, 1981). The clinical material in the preceding chapters is replete with such enactments. Consider the following typical case material:

The 41-year-old man whose nightmares, reportedly "about the war," depicted scenes of being tied and tortured that he had suffered in childhood, but not in combat. The day following the nightmare interview, he left the hospital on pass for an appointment with his parole officer and was jailed because of a urine specimen positive for cocaine (chapter 2, Case 2).

The 44-year-old man with a history of witnessing his mother's numerous sexual infidelities who dreamed of a wartime incident in which he killed two Vietnamese men and a woman. He awoke cross-dressed (chapter 2, Case 3).

The 38-year-old man whose first occurrence of a posttraumatic nightmare took place 12 years after a traumatic sexual assault in jail. He had been homosexually attacked in childhood in the presence of his mother. His demandingness and rage toward male staff members suggested both homosexual yearnings and violent rage and exemplified the type of juggernaut violent behavior that had gotten him repeatedly jailed and exposed him to the trauma of repeated sexual attack (chapter 6).

The 39-year-old recent rape victim who had been evicted from a recovery home on the evening preceding the rape. Before her eviction she had had a "slip dream," then drank, and was evicted. She subsequently left the treatment while she was intoxicated. She believed that she deserved both the eviction and subsequent rape because, in her judgment, she had engineered both situations (chapter 8, Case 1).

Slip dreams: Nightmares about the struggle to resume substance abuse were depicted in the manifest scenario of a number of reported nightmares. These dreams sometimes presaged a return to substance abuse, and, at other times, signaled the temptation to, and imminent danger of, such a relapse that the patient could utilize positively in treatment or recovery efforts (chapter 5, Case 2; chapter 7, Case 5; chapter 8, Case 1; chapter 9, Cases 4, 5, 6).

All these enactments are thought to result from heightened vulnerability, neediness, and fragmentation in the fluid posttraumatic state along with the specific unconscious conflicts with which such a state become associated. They are highly visible and dramatic examples of responses to unconscious conflicts instigated by the posttraumatic state.

The therapist able to utilize the posttraumatic nightmare in a truly psychodynamic fashion, that is, as a true dream, will be better able to address the psychoneurotic difficulties in the latent content; the goal of such a therapeutic focus is to allow the underlying posttraumatic disorder to heal in the context of therapeutic support after the superimposed psychoneurosis has been addressed.

VISTAS

Chapters 2–10 attempted to demonstrate a view of psychopathology informed by nuanced attention to the posttraumatic nightmare. The preceding sections of this chapter have drawn from those psychopathological considerations a point of view on traumatic impact usable by psychotherapists.

The studies of nightmares and the proposed psychotherapeutic model are not intended to be taken at the same level of validity. The studies of the posttraumatic nightmares, detailed and phenomenologically based as they are, have a clinical validity that the psychotherapeutic approach, however informed by this expanded view of psychopathology, does not.

This therapeutic line of thinking aims to expand the purview of psychodynamic psychotherapy to the particular predicament of posttraumatic patients. The posttraumatic nightmare is the centerpiece of—the royal road to, as it were—such an enterprise, since it locates not only the issues of the latent dream content, but also the operations of the dream work that come into play in the construction of the manifest nightmare.

This line of thinking, reclaiming as it does the posttraumatic nightmare for the psychotherapy of posttraumatic patients, does not, of course, substitute for a convincing demonstration of the efficacy of such an approach over others. Nor should it be construed as the basis of a polemic advocating an unmodified and exclusively psychotherapeutic approach to every trauma victim. Such an approach is intended more as a venue to an understanding of issues that compound the impact of trauma; it does not preclude the use of extrapsychotherapeutic modalities as indicated in particular cases. Such modalities include, but are not limited to, medications for mood stabilization and sleep disturbance and to support groups, especially for trauma that results from human malevolence.

In cases in which the trauma represented in the manifest nightmare affects a psyche predisposed by antecedent (childhood) trauma— much of the case material from which the preceding chapters were drawn—the narcissistic retraumatization is severe enough and the shame, dissociation, and affective dysregulation profound enough to necessitate complementing psychodynamic psychotherapy with treatment modalities often deployed in the recovery of substance abusers and adult children of dysfunctional families.

Even though research methodology is beyond the scope of this book, a few comments should be addressed to researchers or research-minded clinicians who would like to think about the ideas presented herein in the context of the methodology of treatment efficacy. The efficacy of any treatment approach remains tentative unless supported by investigation that takes outcome into account.

As is the case with any complex treatment situation, the overall treatment of posttraumatic patients may employ components that find support in demonstrable clinical investigation and research but that, as a clinical totality, form too complex a network of interventions and treatment decisions to be evaluated by the usual research methods.

It is hoped that this book will provide researchers and clinicians alike with precepts that will clarify facets of the posttraumatic clinical picture by the exploration of the posttraumatic nightmare.

Some of the central theses of this book are notable enough to be put to the test as specific falsifiable propositions that can be addressed by systematic research. To name a few:

- ○ Comparison of morbidity and treatment response in trauma due specifically to human malevolence (e.g., rape, mugging, combat) with trauma not due to human malevolence (e.g., auto accidents, natural disasters).
- ○ Comparison of treatment strategies taking the manifest content more or less conclusively at face value with treatment strategies considering the manifest content against the backdrop of predisposing trauma, trauma coexisting with the trauma in the nightmare scenario, and contemporaneous trauma.
- ○ Comparison of treatment focus on the exploration of shame conflicts with those that do not take shame conflicts (and the veiled nature of shame conflicts) into account.
- ○ Comparison of treatment emphasizing psychodynamic psychotherapy that uses the posttraumatic nightmare as a true dream with treatment combinations that do not so utilize the nightmare.

CONCLUSION

The reader has been presented with a series of studies on the post-traumatic nightmare that have broad implications for an expanded understanding of trauma and of posttraumatic states. Implications center on (1) the appreciation of predisposing trauma, especially as shame conflicts sustained from prior and coexisting conflicts affect the traumatic impact of subsequent trauma; (2) the theory of the dynamics of dream formation—in particular, the dynamics of instigation of posttraumatic nightmares and the transformative processes of the dream work whereby both shame and guilt conflicts are transformed into fear in the manifest nightmare scenario; and (3) a model for psychotherapy that focuses on the posttraumatic state with its attendant disorganization and shame as the often veiled accompaniment of more visible symptomatology and the instigator of the posttraumatic nightmare.

These topics have been described and opened, not completed. If the reader takes away an expanded appreciation of the significance of each of these areas and their potential application to the understanding and treatment of the posttraumatic patient, this book will have achieved its purpose.

References

Adams-Silvan, A. & Silvan, M. (1990), A dream is the fulfilment of a wish: Traumatic dream, repetition compulsion, and the pleasure principle. *Internat. J. Psycho-Anal.*, 71:513–522.

American Psychiatric Association (1980), *Diagnostic and statistical manual of mental disorders* (3rd ed.). Washington, DC: American Psychiatric Press.

Behar, D. (1987), Flashbacks and posttraumatic stress symptoms in combat veterans. *Comprehen. Psychiat.*, 28:45–66.

Bion, W R. (1977), *Seven Servants*. New York: Aronson.

Blitz, R. & Greenberg, R. (1984), Nightmares of the traumatic neurosis: Implications for theory and treatment. In: *Psychotherapy of the Combat Veteran,* ed. H. Schwartz. New York: Spectrum, pp. 103–123.

Breger L., Hunter I. & Lane R. W. (1971), The effect of stress on dreams. In: *Preconscious Stimulation in Dreams, Associations, and Images: Classical Studies,* ed. O. Pötzl, R. Allers & J. Teler. *Psychological Issues,* Monogr. 7. New York: International Universities Press.

Breuer, J. & Freud, S. (1893–1895), *Studies on Hysteria. Standard Edition,* 2. London: Hogarth Press, 1955.

Brown, S. (1985), *Treating the Alcoholic.* New York: Wiley.

Burstein, A. (1985), Posttraumatic flashbacks, dream disturbances, and mental imagery. *J. Clin. Psychiat.,* 46:374–378.

Carrol, E. M. & Foy, D. (1992), Assessment and treatment of combat-related post-traumatic stress disorder in a medical center setting. In: *Treating PTSD,* ed. D. Foy. New York: Guilford, pp. 39–68.

Cartwright, R. (1991), Dreams that work: The relation of dream incorporation to adaptation to stressful events. *Dreaming,* 1:3–9.

181

Cohen, J. (1980), Structural consequences of psychic trauma: A new look at "Beyond the Pleasure Principle." *Internat. J. Psycho-Anal.,* 61:421–432.

Dewald, P. (1989), Effects on an adult of incest in childhood. *J. Amer. Psychoanal. Assn.,* 37:992–1114.

Eisnitz, A. (1987), The perspective of the self-representation in dreams. In: *The Interpretations of Dreams and Clinical Work,* ed. A. Rothstein. Madison, CT: International Universities Press, pp. 69–85.

Erikson, E. (1950), *Childhood and Society.* New York. Norton.

Fisher, C., Byrne, J. V., Edwards, A. & Hahn, E. (1970), A psychophysiological study of nightmares. *J. Amer. Psychoanal. Assn.,* 18:747–782.

Fosshage, J. (1983), The psychological function of dreams: A revised psychoanalytic perspective. *Psychoanal. Contemp. Thought,* 6:641–669.

Fox, R. P. (1974), Narcissistic rage and the problem of combat aggression. *Arch. Gen. Psychiat.,* 31:807–811.

Freud, A. (1937), *The Ego and the Mechanisms of Defense.* New York: International Universities Press.

Freud, S. (1899), Screen memories. *Standard Edition,* 3:301–322. London: Hogarth Press, 1962.

_____ (1900), *The Interpretation of Dreams. Standard Edition.* 4 & 5. London: Hogarth Press, 1953.

_____ (1905), *Three Essays on the Theory of Sexuality. Standard Edition,* 7:130–245. London: Hogarth Press, 1953.

_____ (1916a) Some character-types met with in psycho-analytic work. *Standard Edition,* 14:309–333. London: Hogarth Press, 1957.

_____ (1916b), *Introductory Lectures on Psycho-Analysis: Part II. Dreams. Standard Edition,* 15. London: Hogarth Press, 1963.

_____ (1917), A metapsychological supplement to the theory of dreams. *Standard Edition,* 14:217–235. London: Hogarth Press, 1957.

_____ (1918), From the history of an infantile neurosis. *Standard Edition,* 17:7–122. London: Hogarth Press, 1955.

_____ (1919), The uncanny. *Standard Edition,* 17:217–256. London: Hogarth Press, 1955.

_____ (1920), *Beyond the Pleasure Principle. Standard Edition,* 18:7–64. London: Hogarth Press, 1955.

_____ (1930), Civilization and its discontents, *Standard Edition,* 21:64–145. London: Hogarth Press, 1961.

_____ (1933), *New Introductory Lectures on Psycho-analysis. Standard Edition,* 22:5–182. London: Hogarth Press, 1964.

Glover, E. (1929), The screening function of traumatic memories. *Internat. J. Psycho-Anal.,* 10:90–93.

Green, A. (1977), The borderline concept: A conceptual framework for the understanding of borderline patients: Suggested hypotheses. In: *Borderline Personality Disorders,* ed. P. Hartocollis. New York: International Universities Press, pp. 115–144.

Greenson, R. (1954), The struggle against identification. *J. Amer. Psychoanal. Assn.,* 2:200–217.

Grigsby, J. P. (1987), The use of imagery in the treatment of posttraumatic stress disorder. *J. Nerv. Ment. Dis.,* 175:55–59.

Grinstein, A. (1983), *Freud's Rules of Dream Interpretation.* New York: International Universities Press.

Hartmann, E. (1984), *The Nightmare.* New York: Basic Books.

———— (1991), Dreams that work or dreams that poison? What does dreaming do: An editorial essay. *Dreaming,* 1:23–26.

Herman, J. (1992), *Trauma and Recovery.* New York: Basic Books.

Hersen, M. (1971), Personality characteristics of nightmare sufferers. *J. Nerv. Ment. Dis.,* 153:27–31.

Hobson, J. (1988), *The Dreaming Brain.* New York: Basic Books.

Horowitz, M. J. (1969), Flashbacks: Recurrent intrusive images after the use of LSD. *Amer. J. Psychiat.,* 126:565–569.

Jones, E. (1910), *On the Nightmare.* London: Hogarth Press, 1951.

Kernberg, O. F. (1984), *Severe Personality Disorders.* New Haven, CT: Yale University Press.

Kohut, H. (1971), *The Analysis of the Self.* New York: International Universities Press.

———— (1977), *The Restoration of the Self.* New York: International Universities Press.

Kramer, M. (1991), The nightmare: A failure in dream function. *Dreaming,* 1:277–285.

———— Schoen, L. S., Kinney, L. (1987), Nightmares in Vietnam veterans. *J. Amer. Acad. Psychoanal.,* 15:67–81.

Kris, A. (1975), On wanting too much: Freud's exceptions revisited. *Internat. J. Psycho-Anal.,* 56:85–95.

Kubie, L. S. (1939), A critical analysis of the concept of a repetition compulsion. *Internat. J. Psycho-Anal.,* 20:390–402.

Lansky, M. R. (1977), Establishing a family-oriented inpatient unit. *J. Operational Psychiat.,* 8:66–74.

———— (1984), The family treatment program at Brentwood V.A. Medical Center. *Family Systems Med.,* 2:102–106.

———— (1985), Preoccupation and pathologic distance regulation. *Internat. J. Psychoanal. Psychother.,* 11:409–426.

———— (1988), The subacute hospital treatment of the borderline patient: I. An educational component. *Hillside J. Clin. Psychiat.,* 10:24–37.

———— (1989), The subacute hospital treatment of the borderline patient: III. Management of suicidal crisis by family intervention. *Hillside J. Clin. Psychiat.,* 11:81–97.

———— (1992a), *Fathers Who Fail.* Hillsdale, NJ: The Analytic Press.

———— ed. (1992b), *Essential Papers on Dreams.* New York: New York University Press.

———— & Morrison, A. P. (in press), Shame in Freud's writings. In: *The Range of Shame,* ed. M. R. Lansky & A. P. Morrison. Hillsdale, NJ: The Analytic Press.

Lavie, P. & Kaminer, H. (1991), Dreams that poison sleep: Dreaming in Holocaust survivors. *Dreaming,* 1:11–22.

Leveton, A. (1961), The night residue. *Internat. J. Psycho-Anal.,* 42:506–516.

Levin, S. (1967), Some metapsychological considerations on the differentiation between shame and guilt. *Internat. J. Psycho-Anal.,* 48:267–276.

Lewis, H. B. (1971), *Shame and Guilt in Neurosis.* New York: International Universities Press.

───── ed. (1987), *The Role of Shame in Symptom Formation.* Hillsdale, NJ: Lawrence Erlbaum Associates.

Lidz, T. (1946), Nightmares and combat neuroses. *Psychiat.,* 19:37–49.

Lipin, T. (1963), Repetition compulsion and maturational drive-representatives. *Internat. J. Psycho-Anal.,* 44:398–406.

Mack, J. (1965), Nightmares, conflict and ego development in chilhdood. *Internat. J. Psycho-Anal.,* 46:403–428.

───── (1970), *Nightmares and Human Conflict.* Boston: Houghton Mifflin.

Mellman, T. A. & Davis, G. C. (1985), Combat-related flashbacks in posttraumatic stress disorder: Phenomenology and similarity to panic attacks. *J. Clin. Psychiat.,* 46:379–382.

Moses, R. (1978), Adult psychic trauma: The question of early predisposition. *Internat. J. Psycho-Anal.,* 59:353–363.

Nietzsche, F. (1888), *Thus Spake Zarathustra.* Staten Island, NY: Gordon Press.

Oremland, J.D. (1987), Dreams in the treatment of the borderline personality. In: *The Borderline Patient,* Vol. 2, ed. J. S. Grotstein, M. F. Solomon & J. A. Lang. Hillsdale, NJ: The Analytic Press, pp. 81–101.

Ornstein, P. H. (1987), On self-state dreams in the psychoanalytic treatment process. In: *The Interpretations of Dreams in Clinical Work,* ed A. Rothstein. Madison, CT: International Universities Press, pp. 87–104.

Piers, G. & Singer, M. (1953), *Shame and Guilt.* New York: Norton.

Rangell, L. (1954), The psychology of poise: With special elaboration on the psychic significance of the snout or perioral region. *Internat. J. Psycho-Anal.,* 35:313–333.

───── (1967), The metapsychology of psychic trauma. In: *Psychic Trauma,* ed. S. Furst. New York: Basic Books, pp. 51–84.

Reed, G. S. (1987), Rules of clinical understanding in classical psychoanalysis and in self psychology: A comparison. *J. Amer. Psychoanal. Assn.,* 35:421–446.

Roth, N. (1958), Manifest dream content and acting out. *Psychoanal. Quart.,* 27:547–553.

Saidel, D. R. & Babineau, R. (1976), Prolonged LSD flashbacks as conversion reactions. *J. Nerv. Ment. Dis.,* 163:352–355.

Scheff, T. (1987), The shame-rage spiral: A case study of an interminable quarrel. In: *The Role of Shame in Symptom Formation,* ed. H. B. Lewis. Hillsdale, NJ: Lawrence Erlbaum Associates, pp. 109–150.

───── (1990), *Microsociology.* Chicago: University of Chicago Press.

Segal, H. (1981), The function of dreams. In: *Do I Dare Disturb the Universe?* ed. J. Grotstein. Beverly Hills, CA: Caesura Press, pp. 579–588.

Slap, J. W. & Trunnell, E. E. (1987), Reflections on the self-state dream. *Psychoanal. Quart.,* 61:251–262.

Terr, L. (1991), Childhood traumas: An outline and overview. *Amer. J. Psychoanal.,* 148:10–20.

van der Kolk, B., Blitz, R., Burr, W., Sherry, S. & Hartmann, E. (1984), Nightmares and trauma: A comparison of nightmares after combat with lifelong nightmares. *Amer. J. Psychiat.,* 141:187–190.

Weiss, J. & Sampson, H. (1986), *The Psychoanalytic Process.*. New York: Guilford.

Wisdom, J. O. (1949), A hypothesis to explain trauma reenactment dreams. *Internat. J. Psycho-Anal.,* 31:13–20.

Zulliger, H. (1934), Prophetic dreams. *Internat. J. Psycho-Anal.,* 15:191–208.

Index